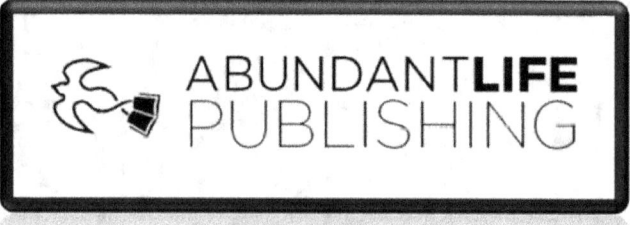

Copyright © 2018

Abundant Life Publishing

All Rights Reserved.

No part of this book may be reproduced in any form without permission in writing from the publisher, except in the case of brief quotations embodied in critical articles or reviews.

Edited by: Gavriela Powers

Cover and Interior Design: Gavriela Powers

We hope you enjoy this book from Abundant Life Publishing.

Our goal is to help you and your little ones live, laugh, and be the light of Yeshua (Jesus)!

Abundant Life Publishing

Salisbury, NC

Printed in the United States of America

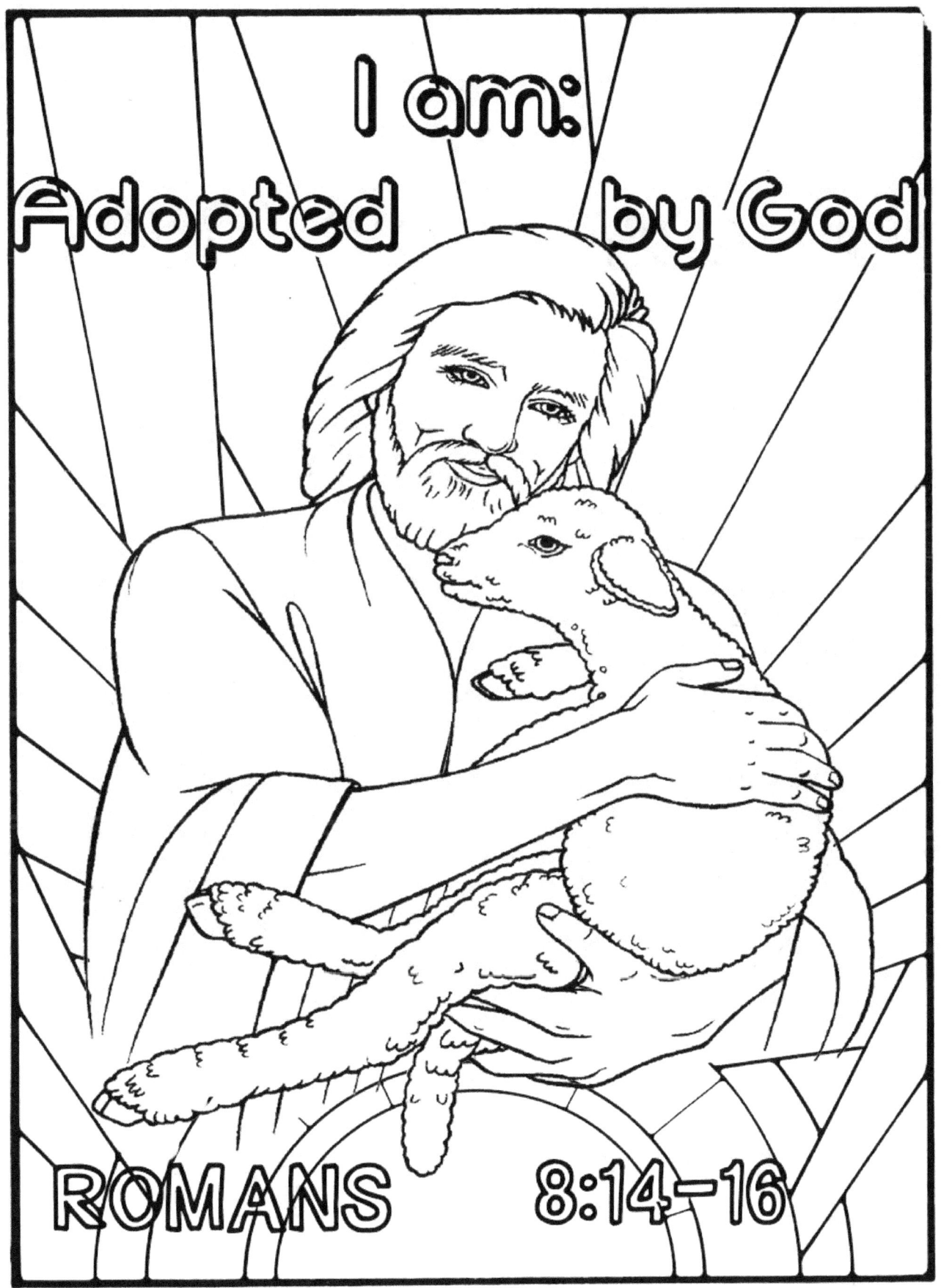

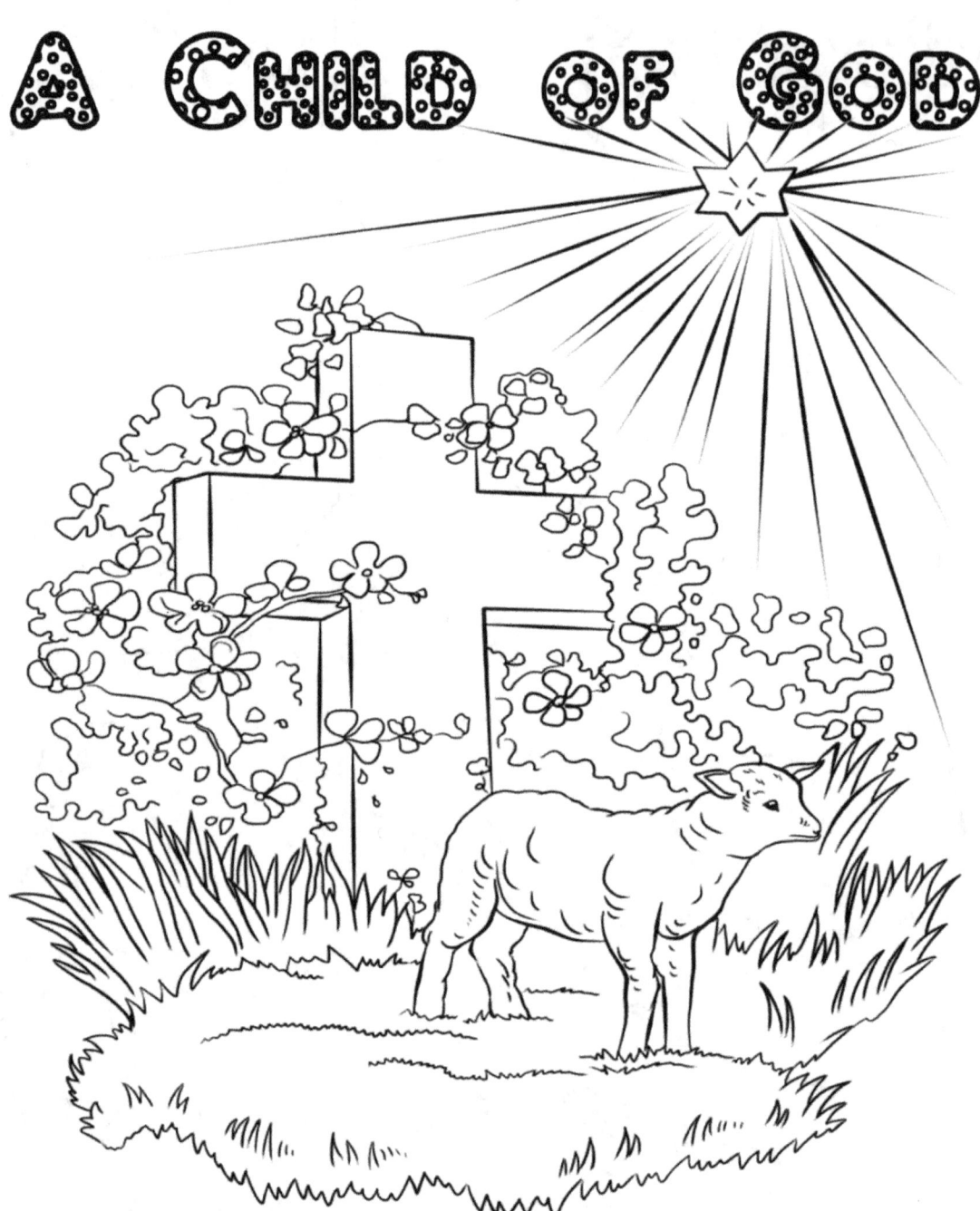

I am: A Priest

REVELATION 1:6

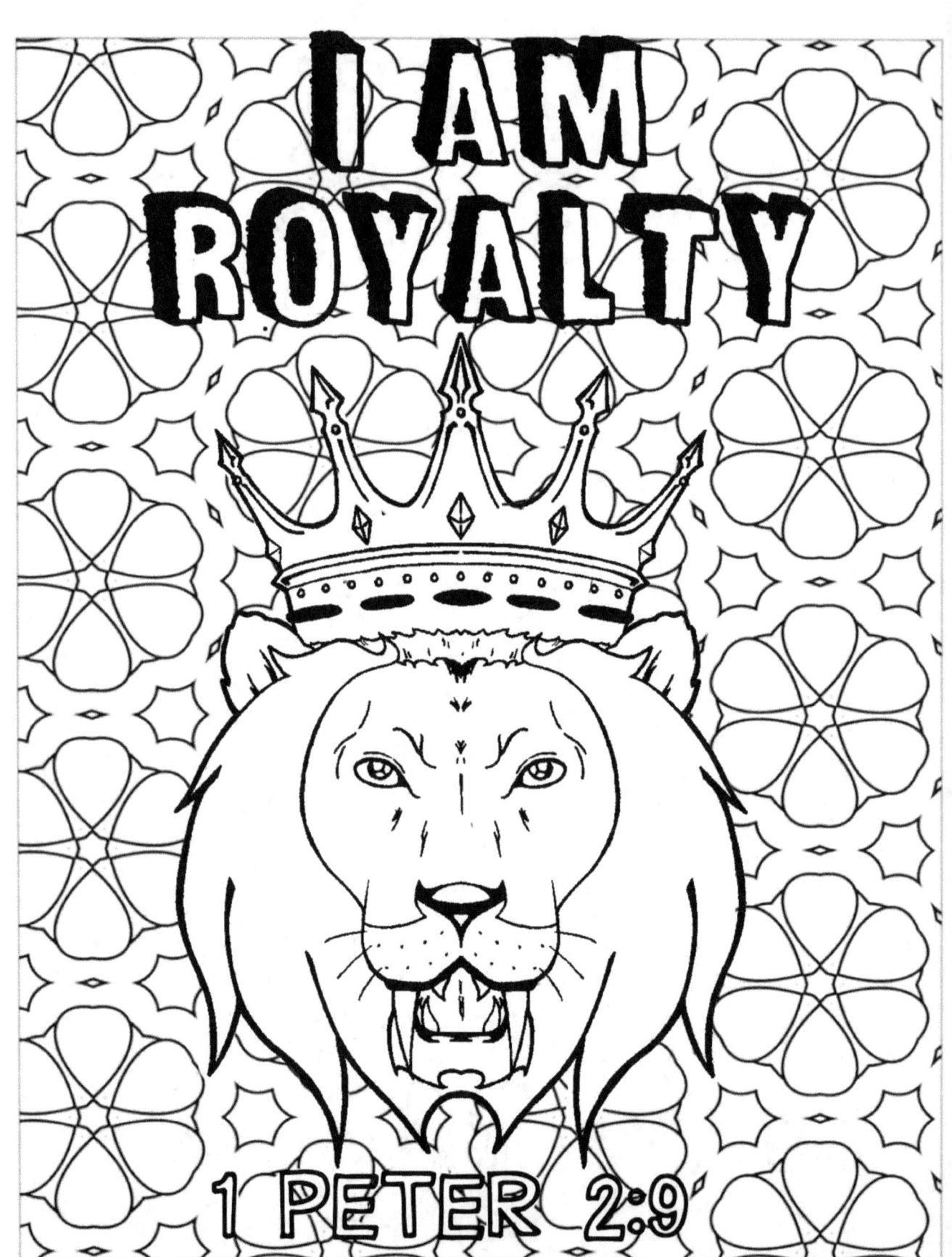

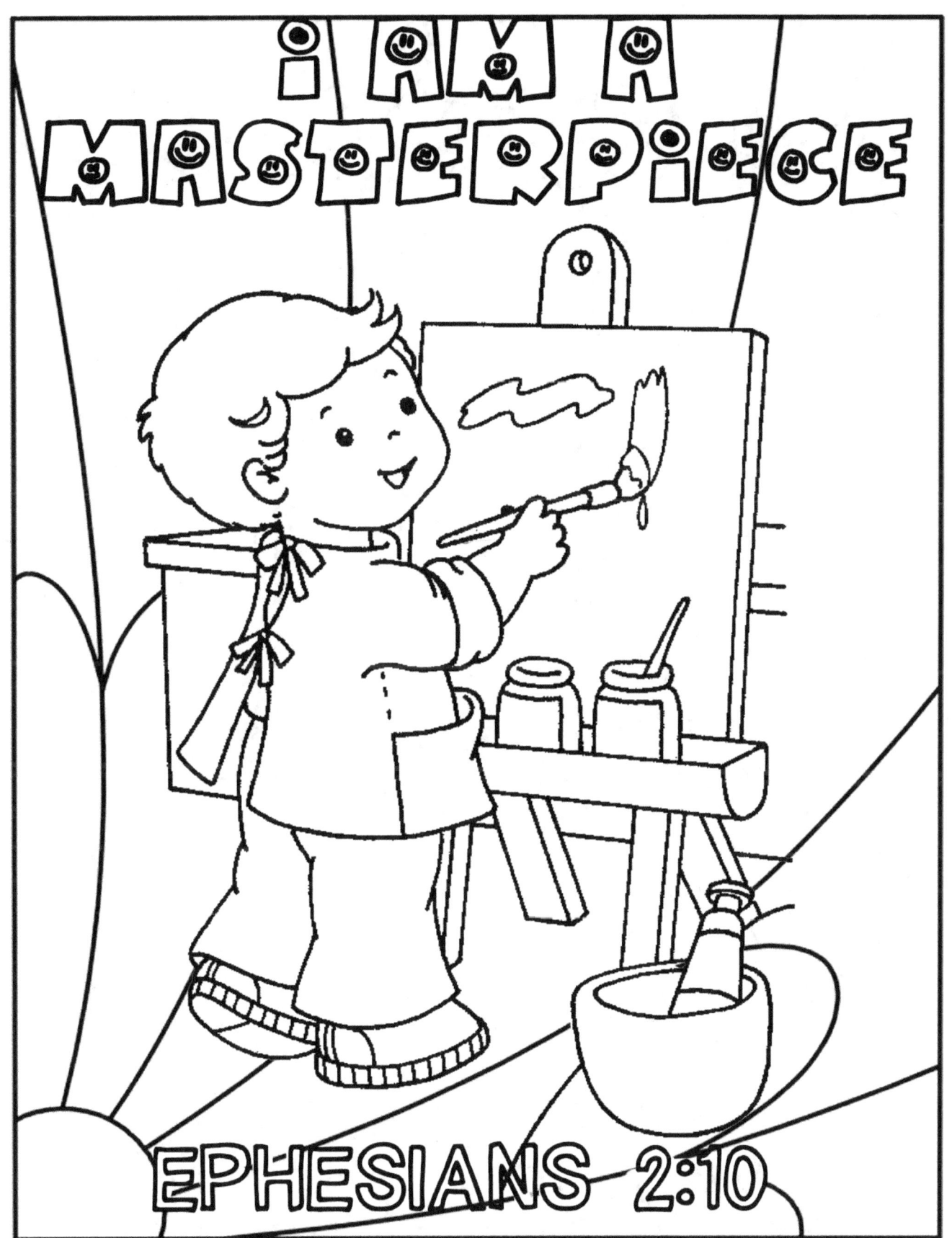

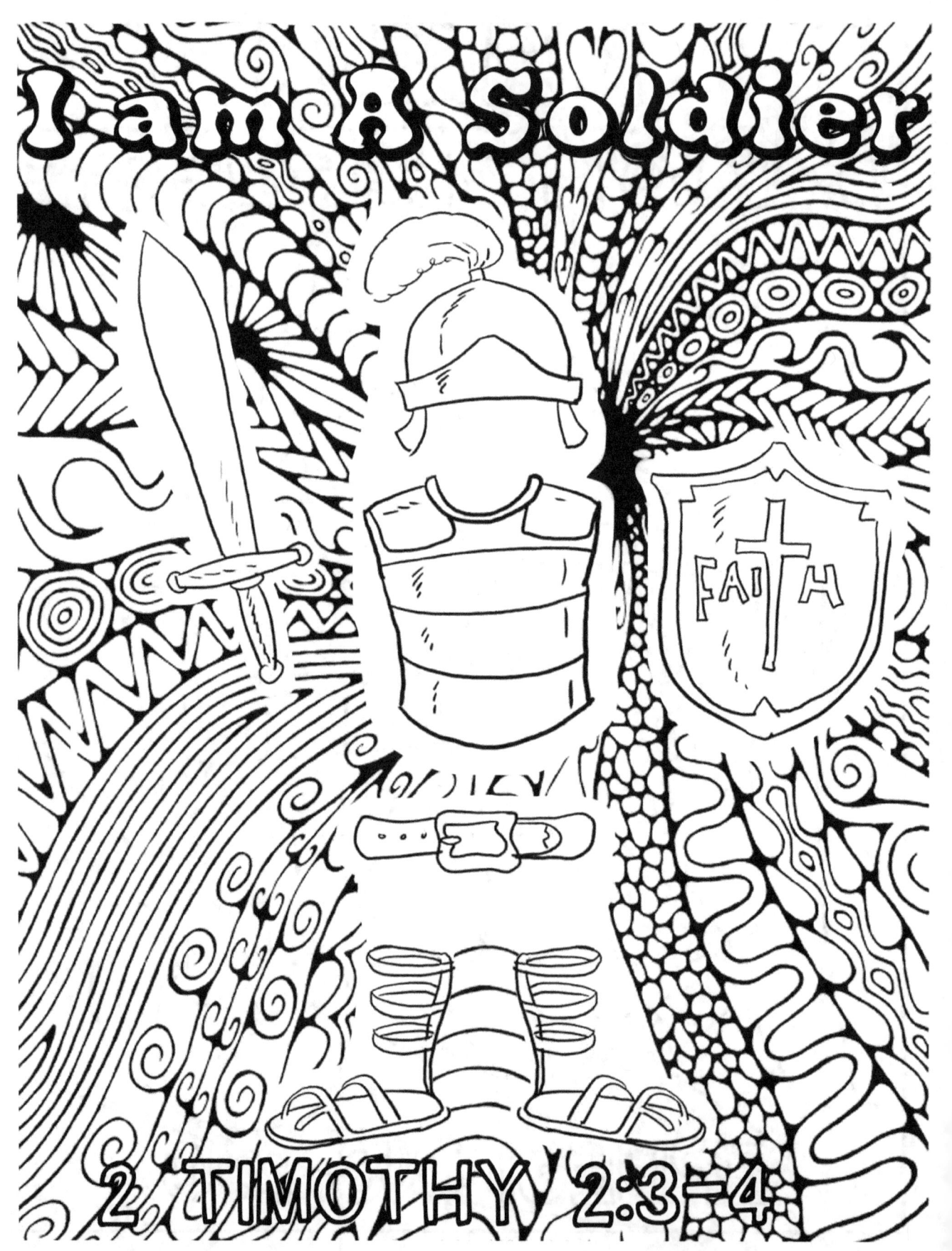

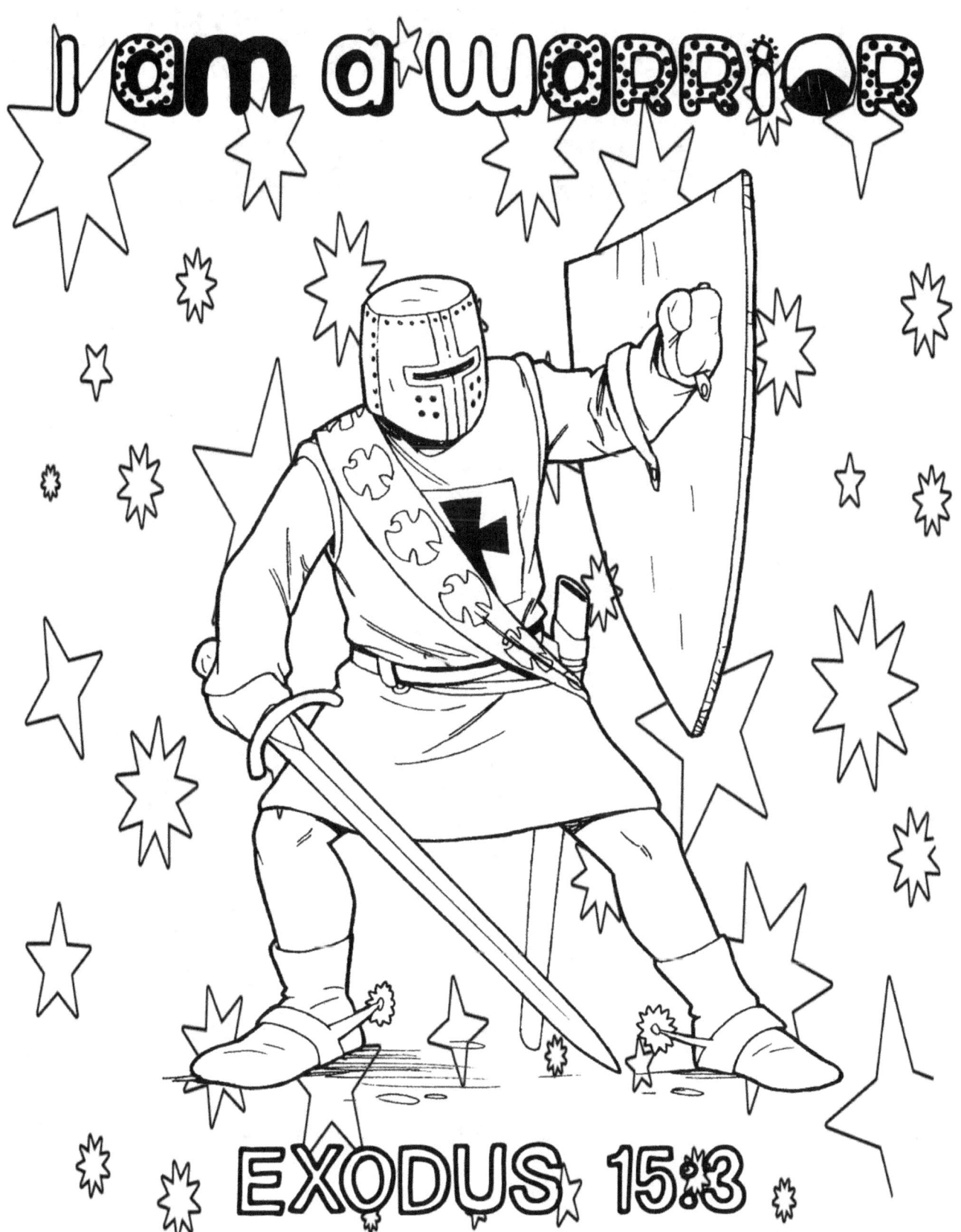

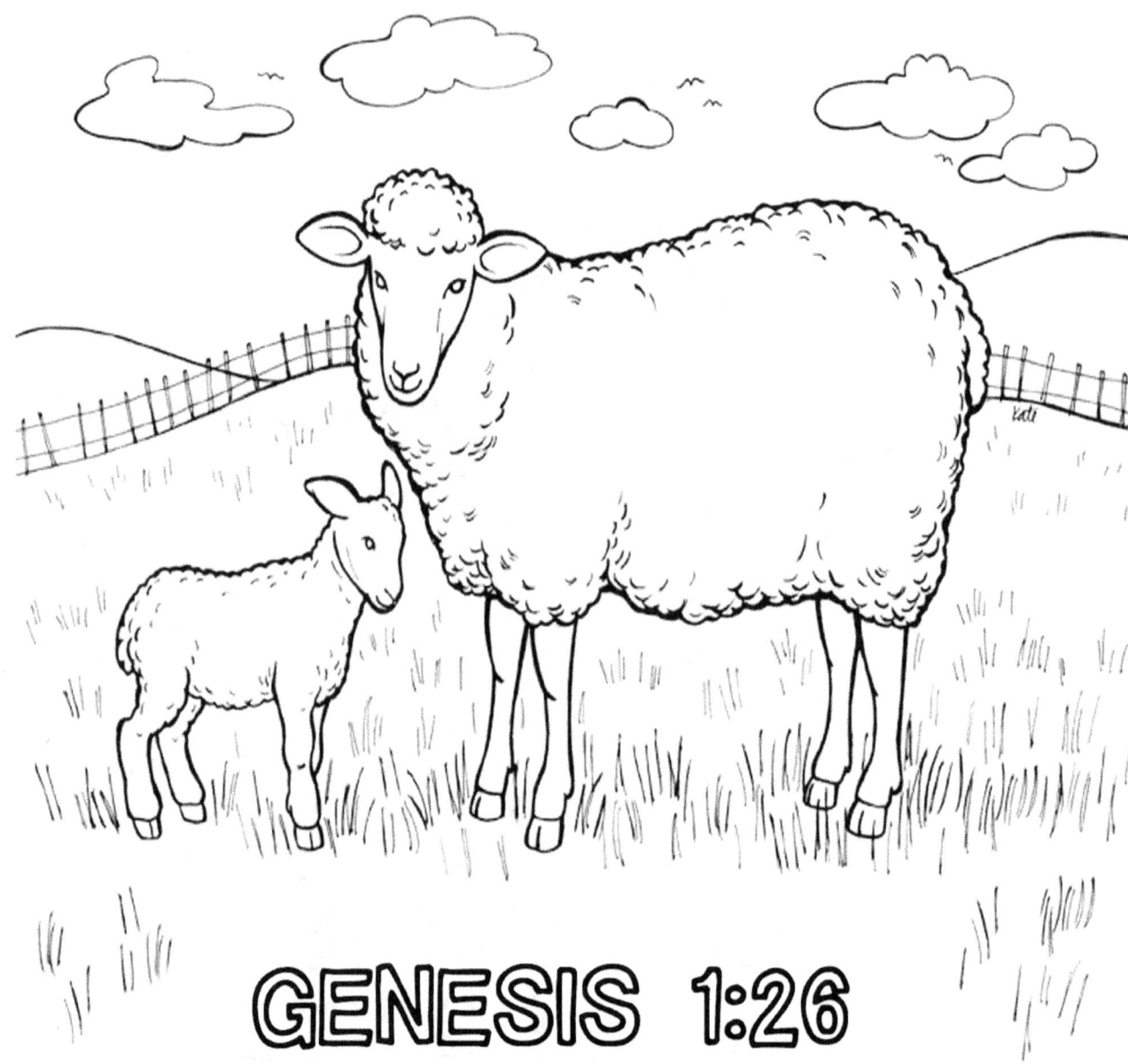

i am a Saint

ROMANS 1:7

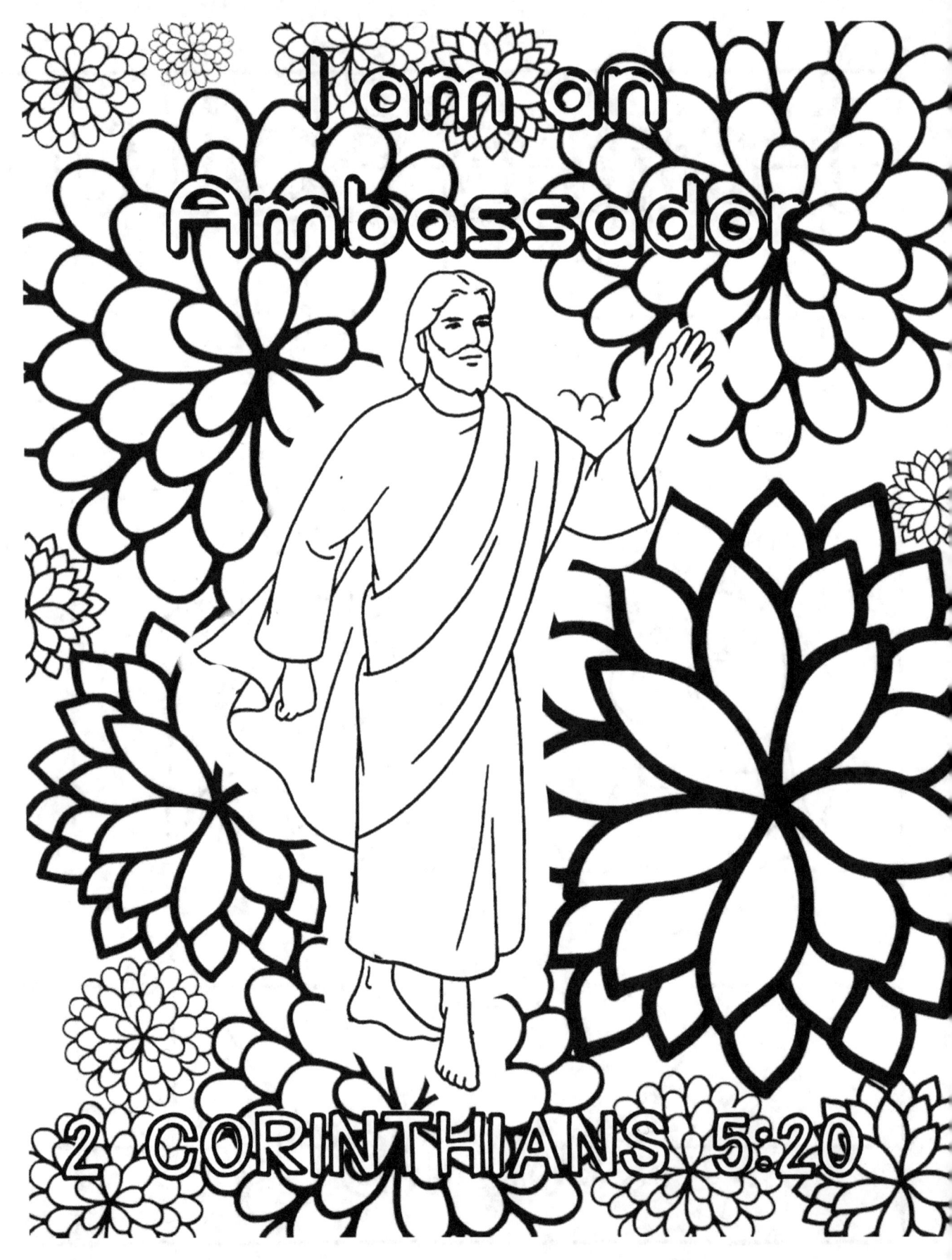

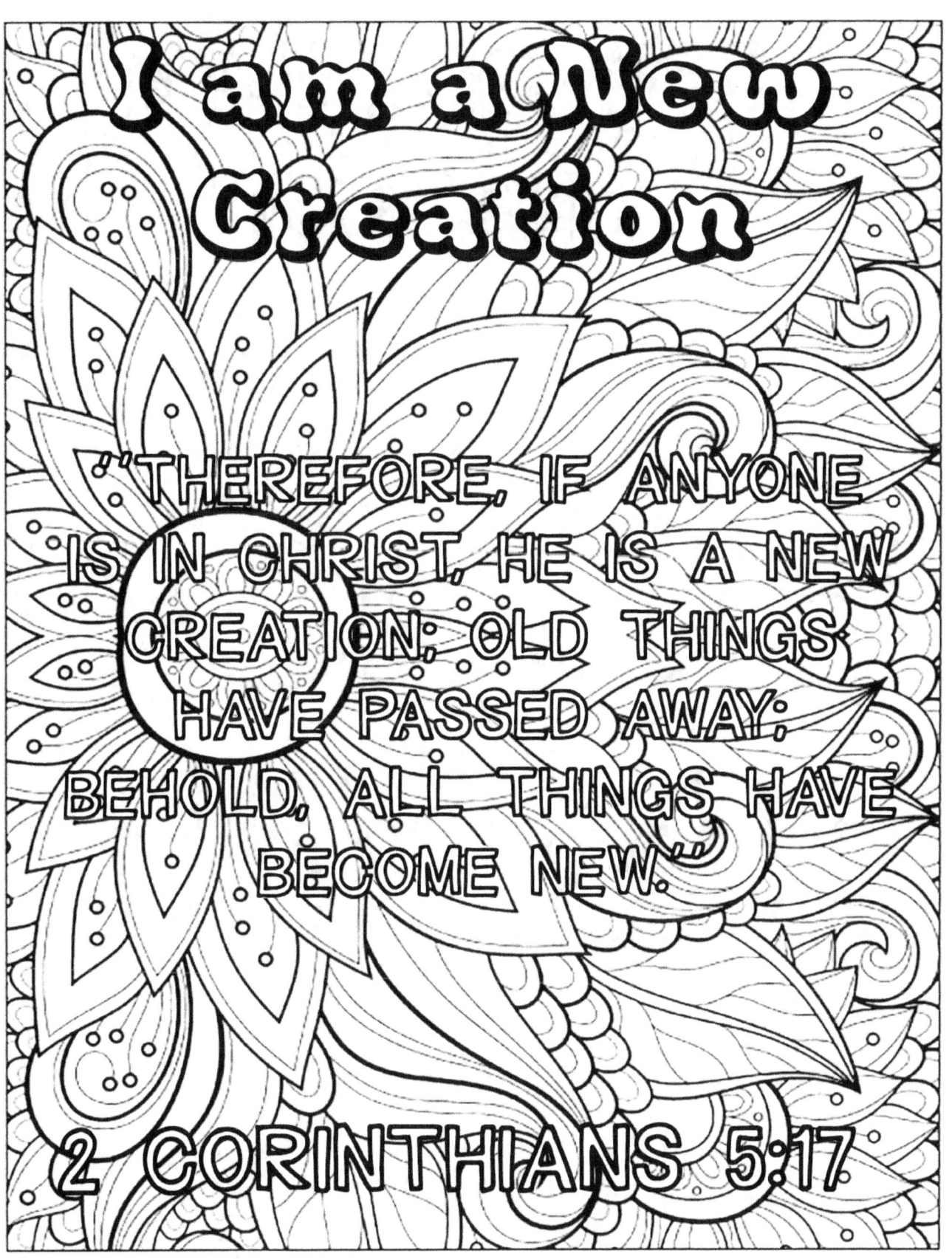

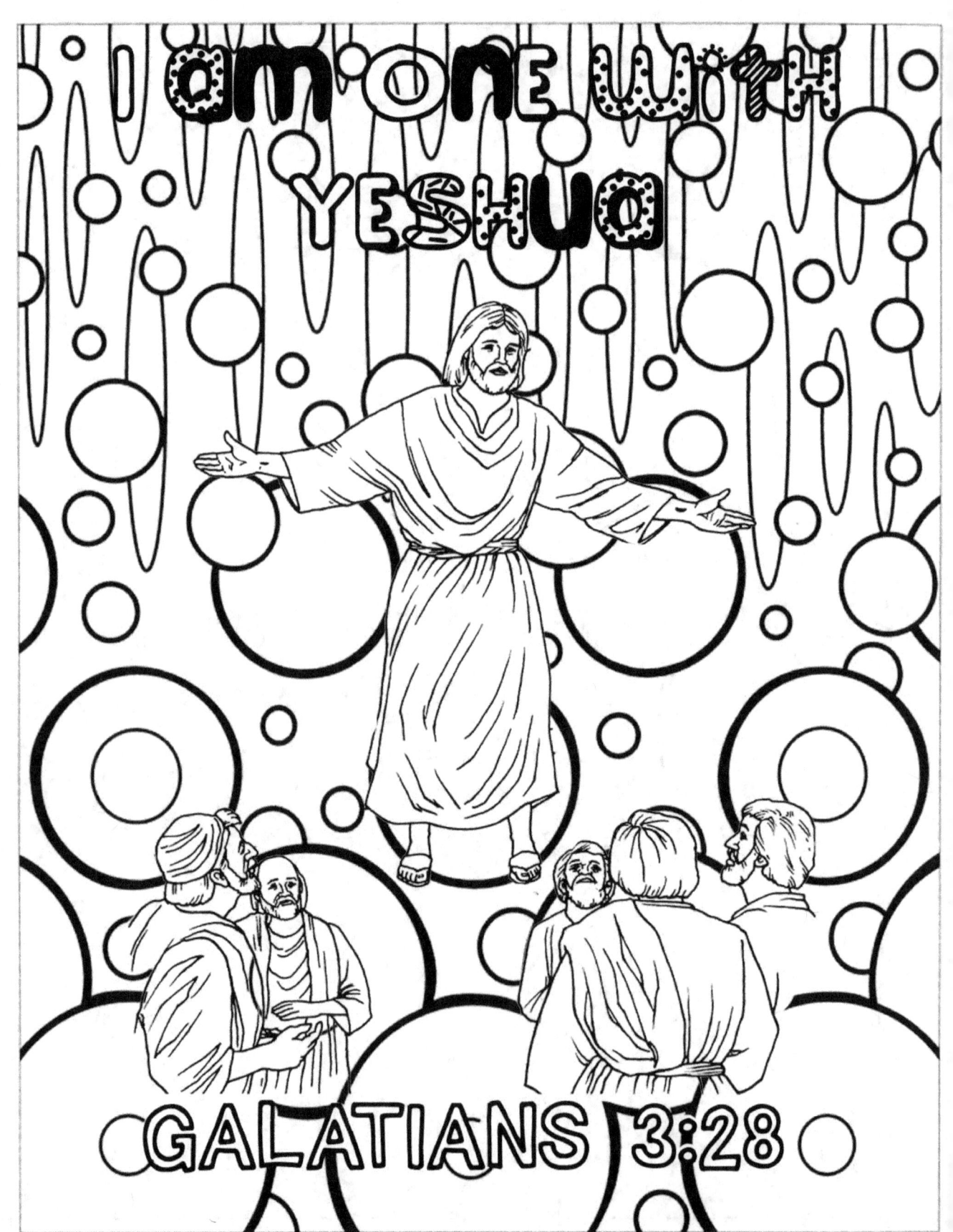

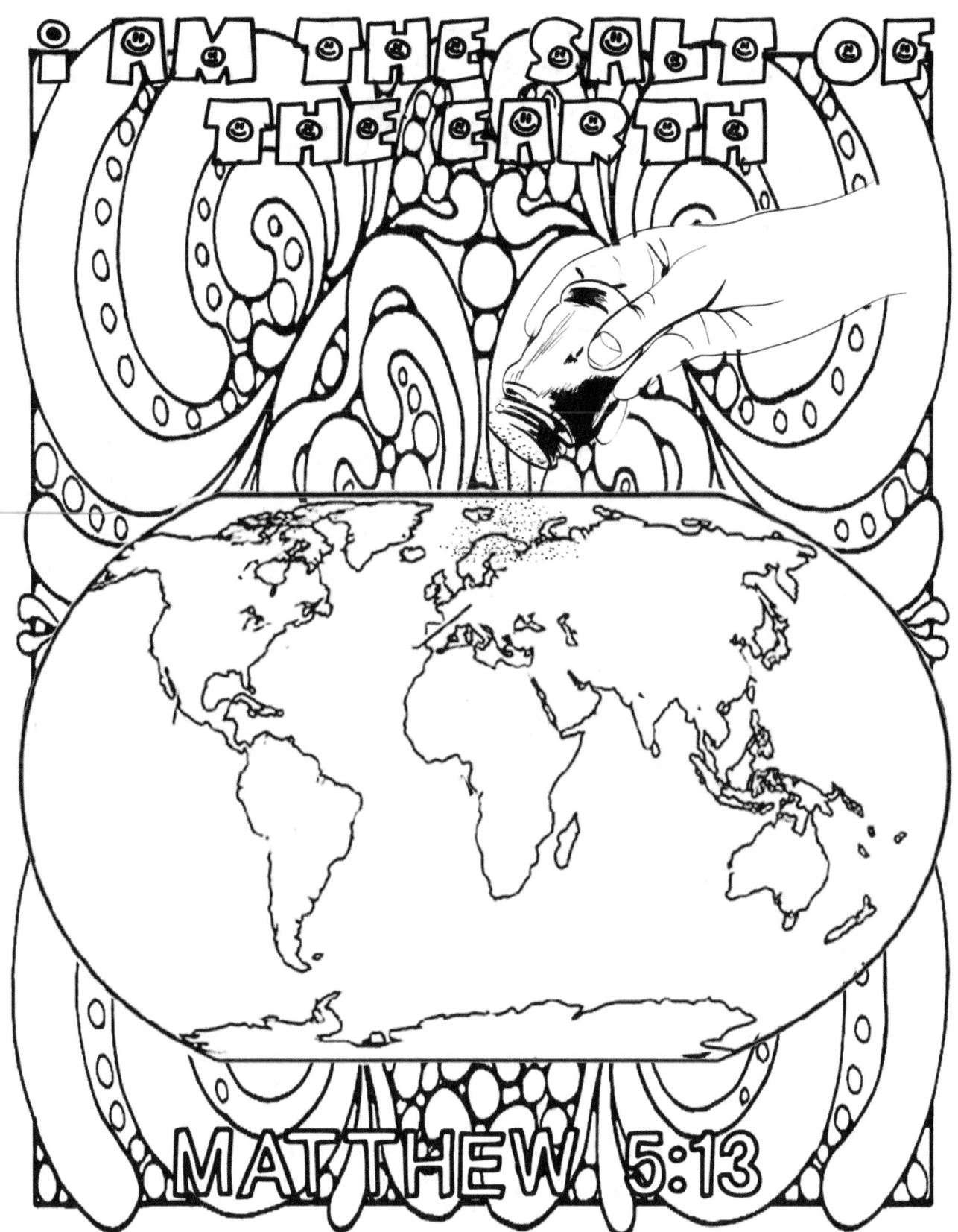

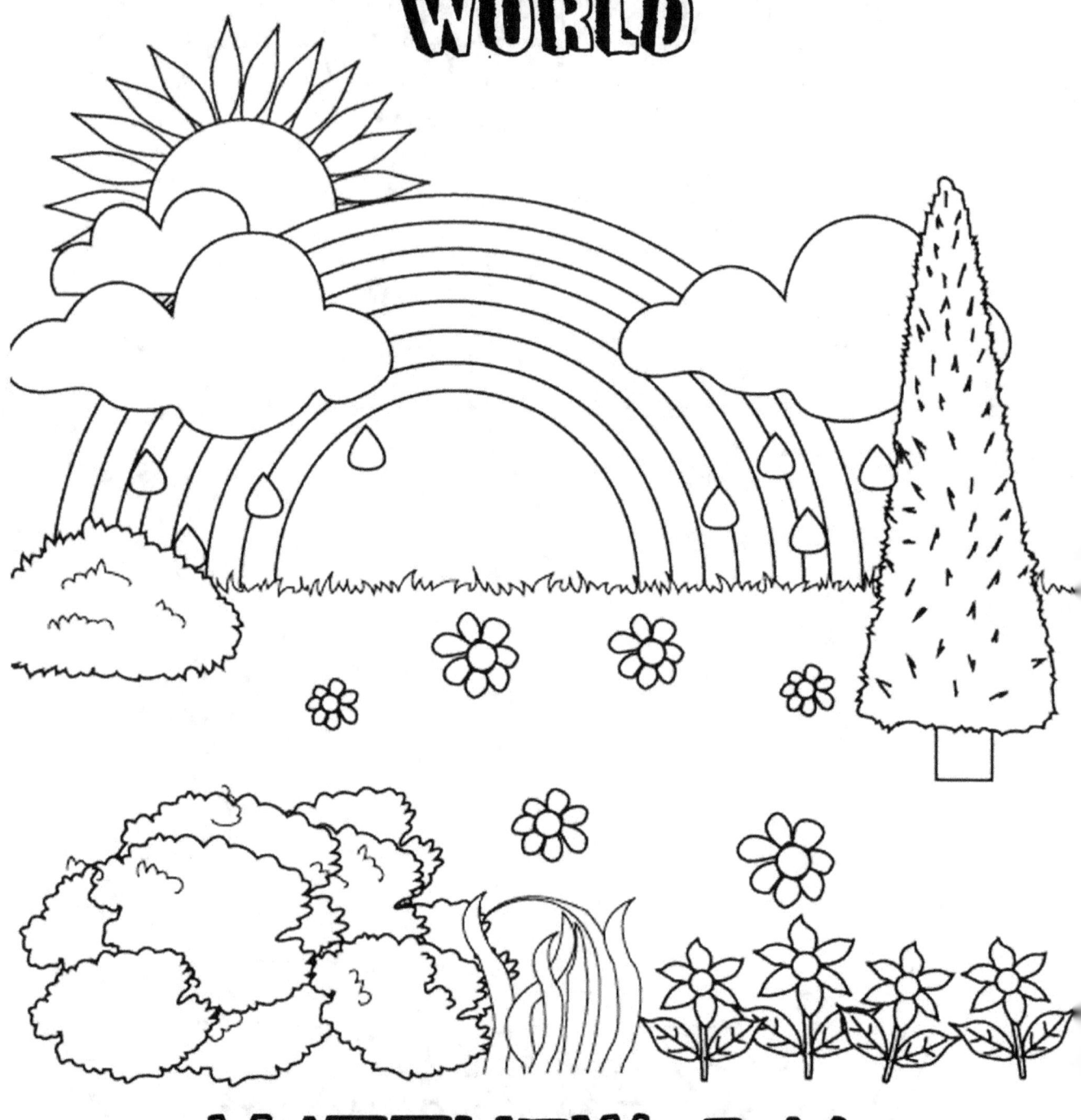

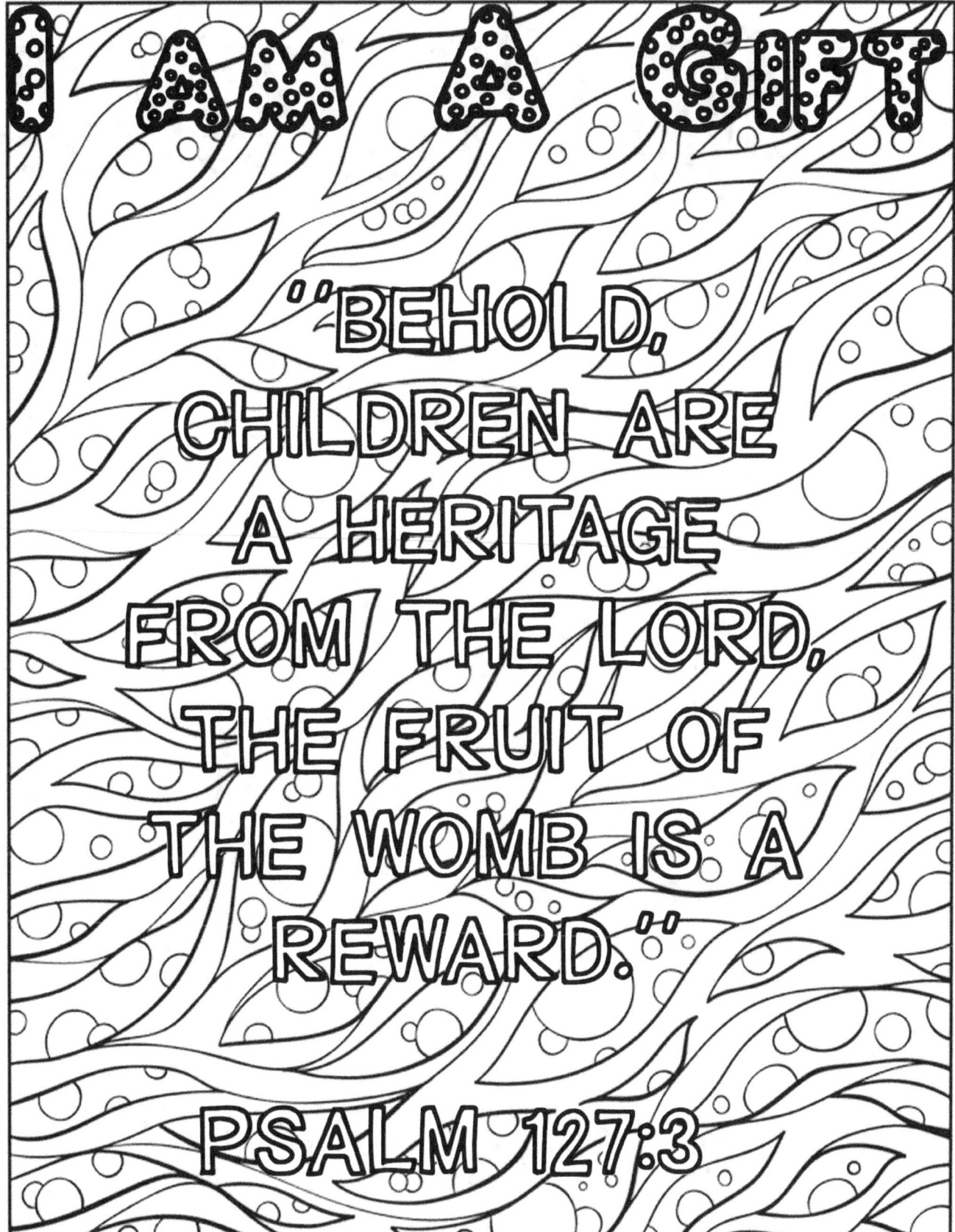

i AM POWERFUL

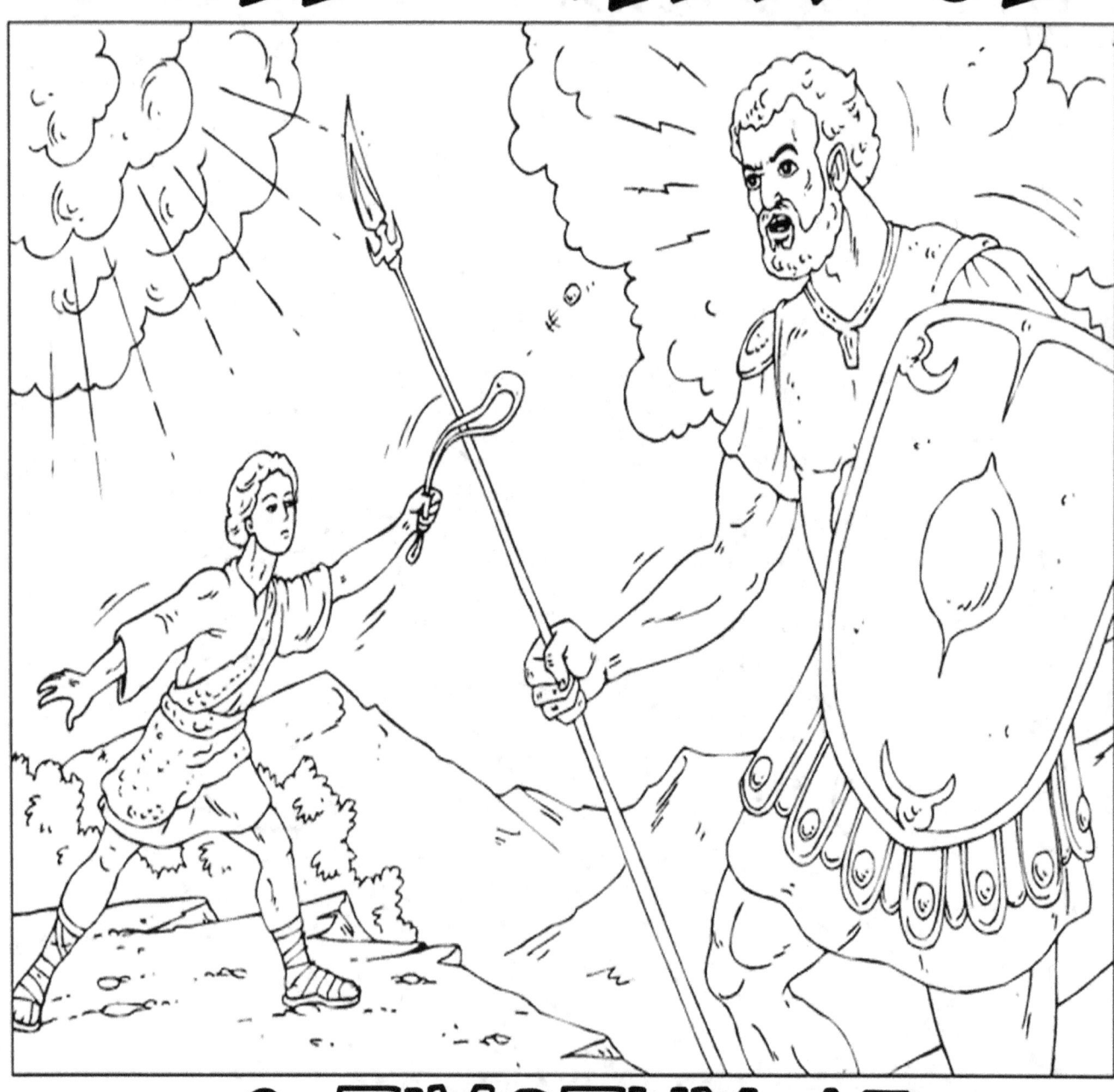

2 TIMOTHY 1:7

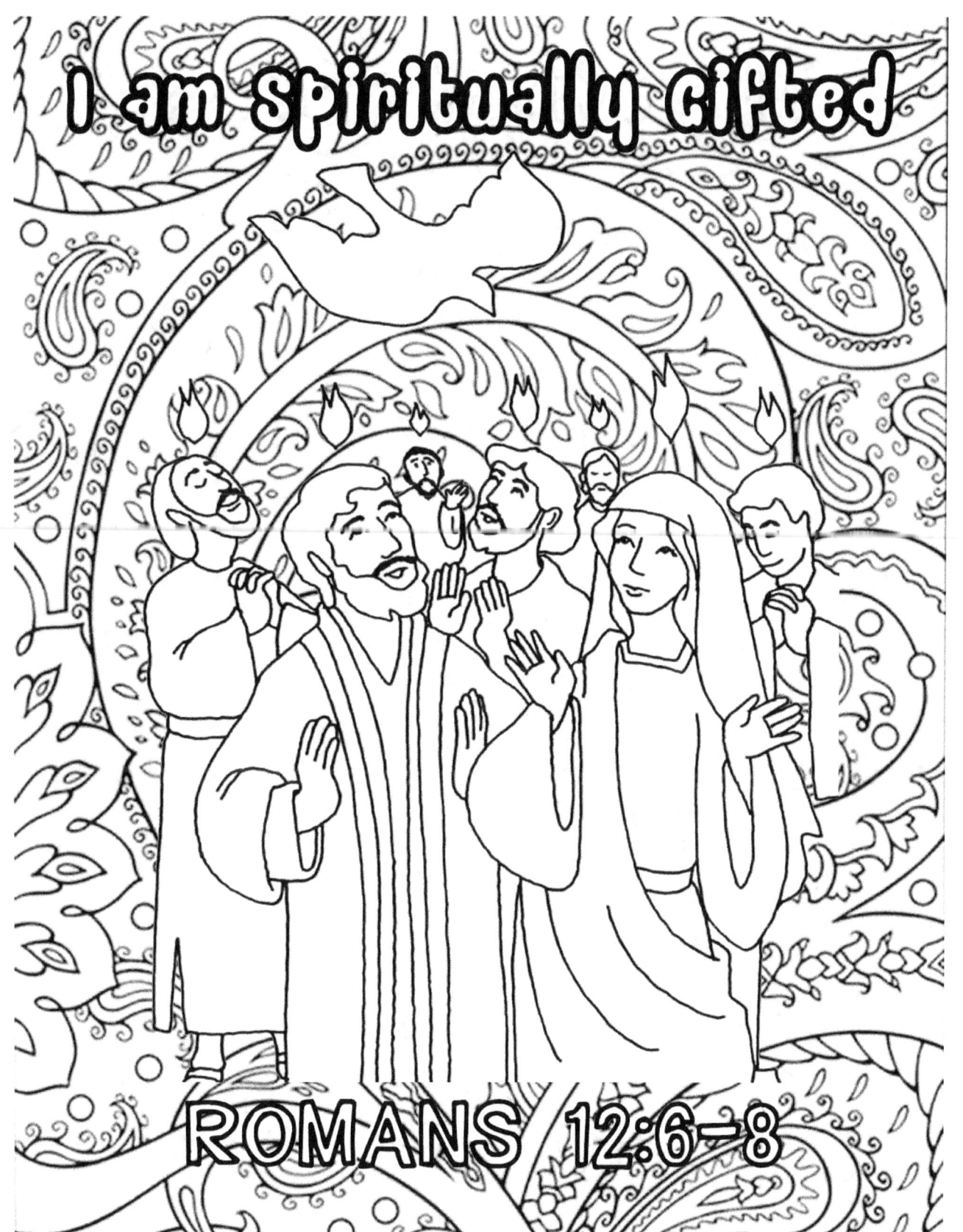

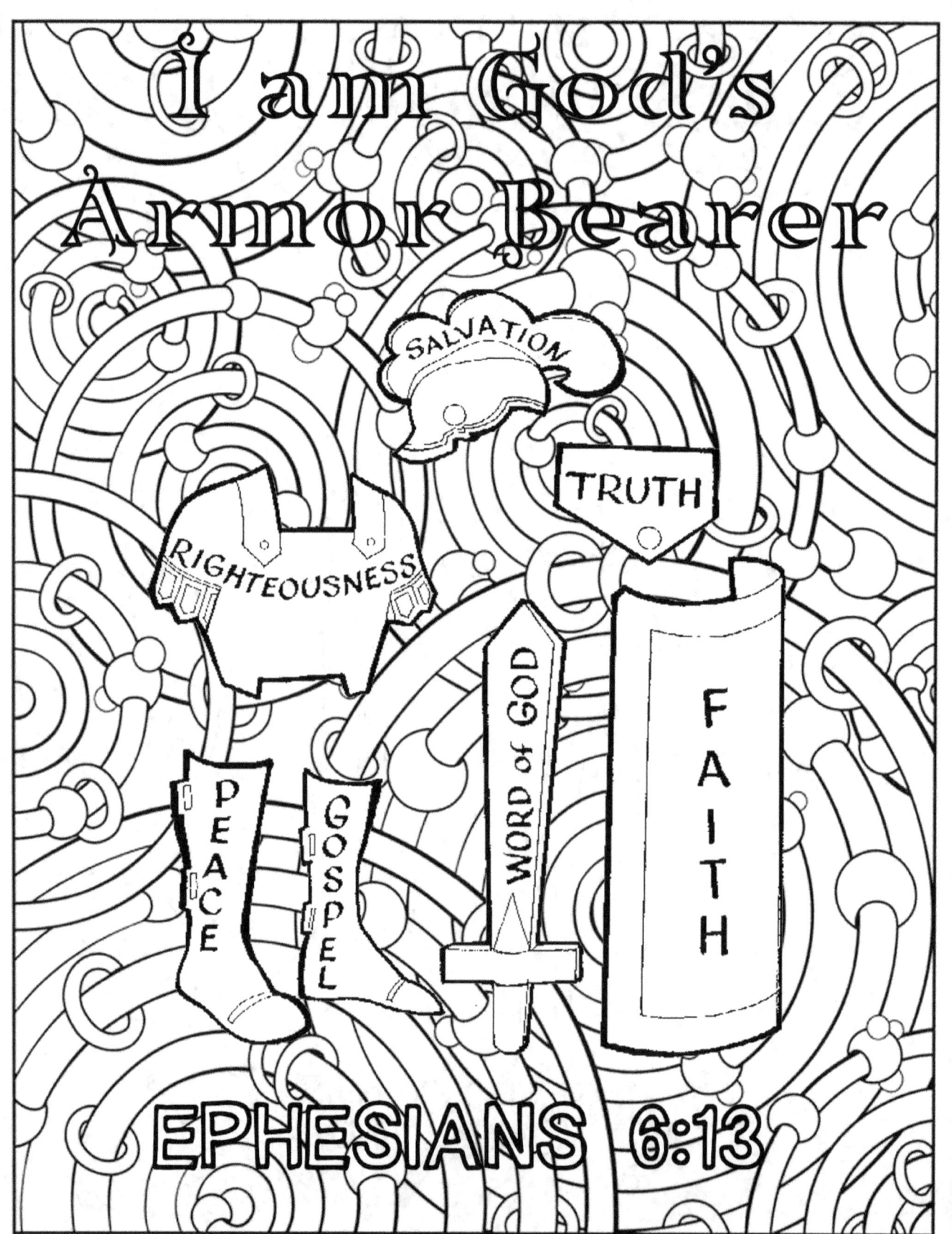

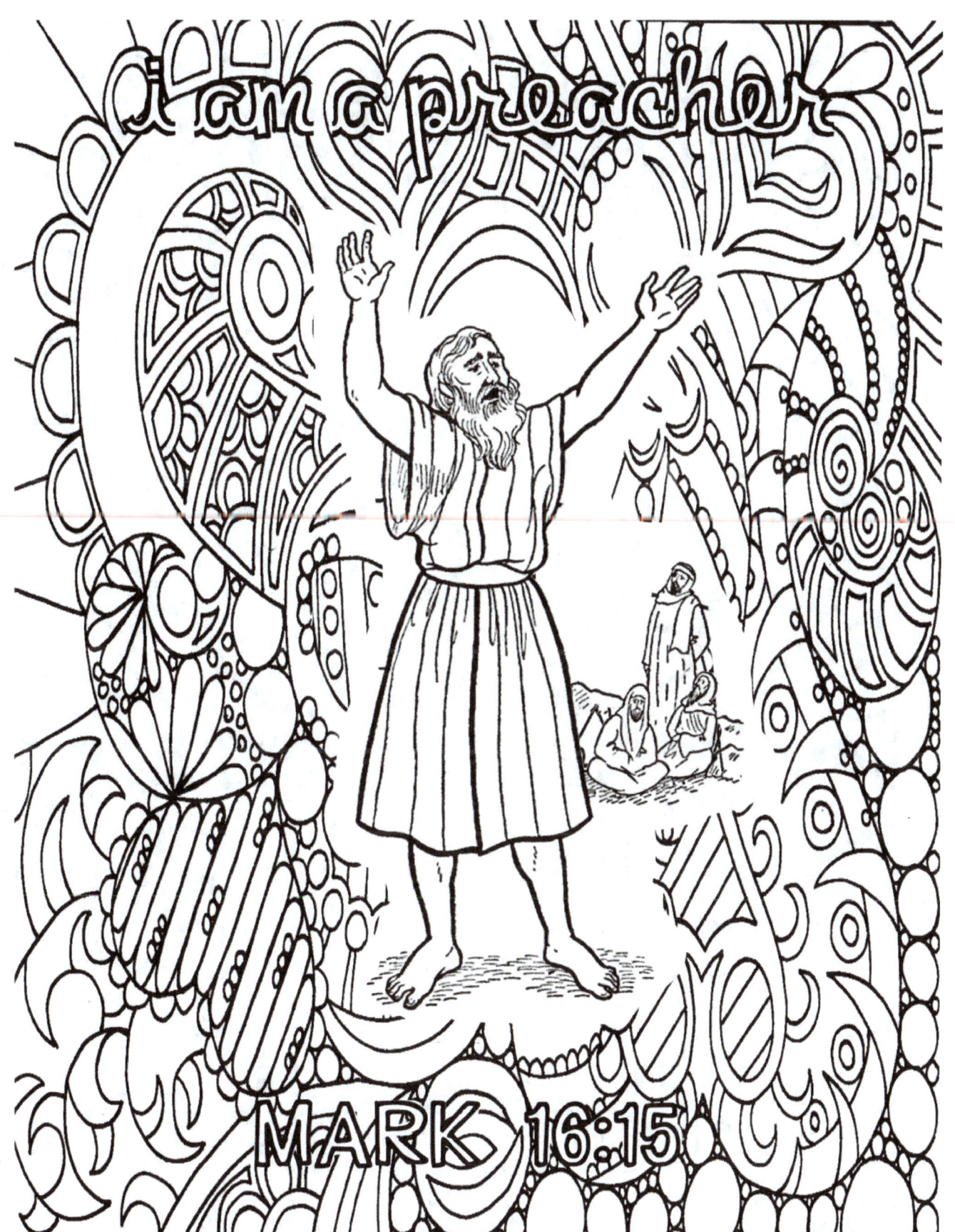

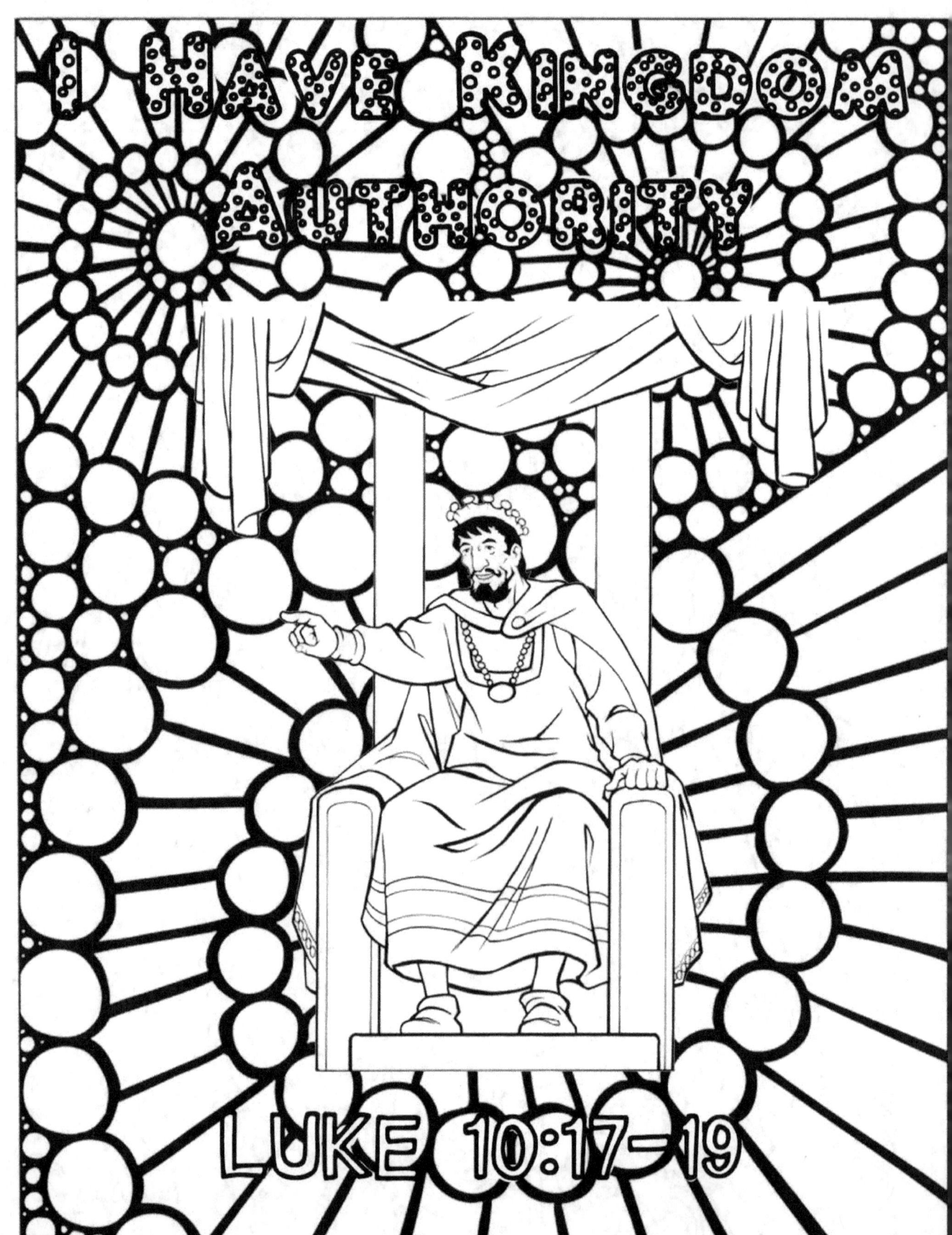

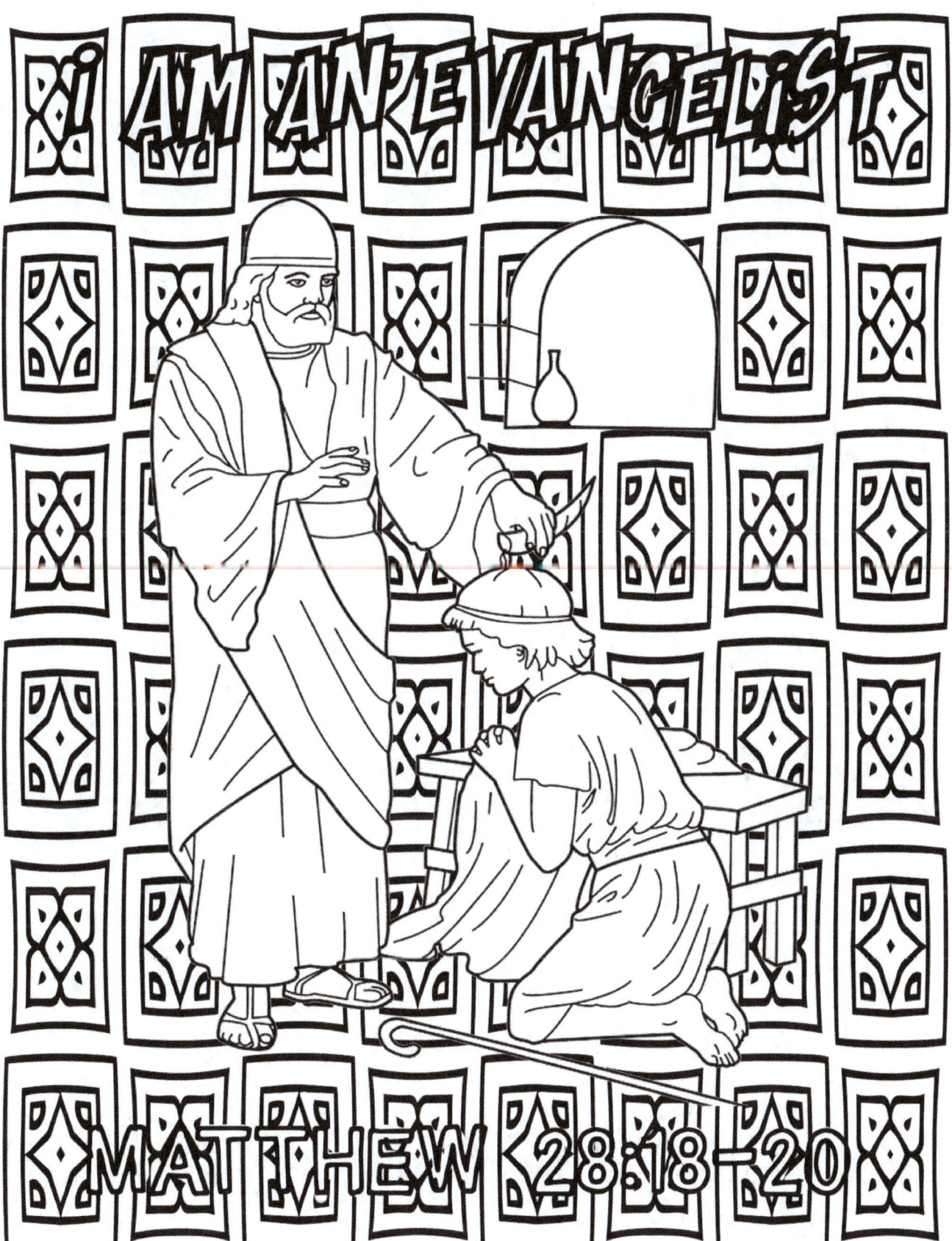

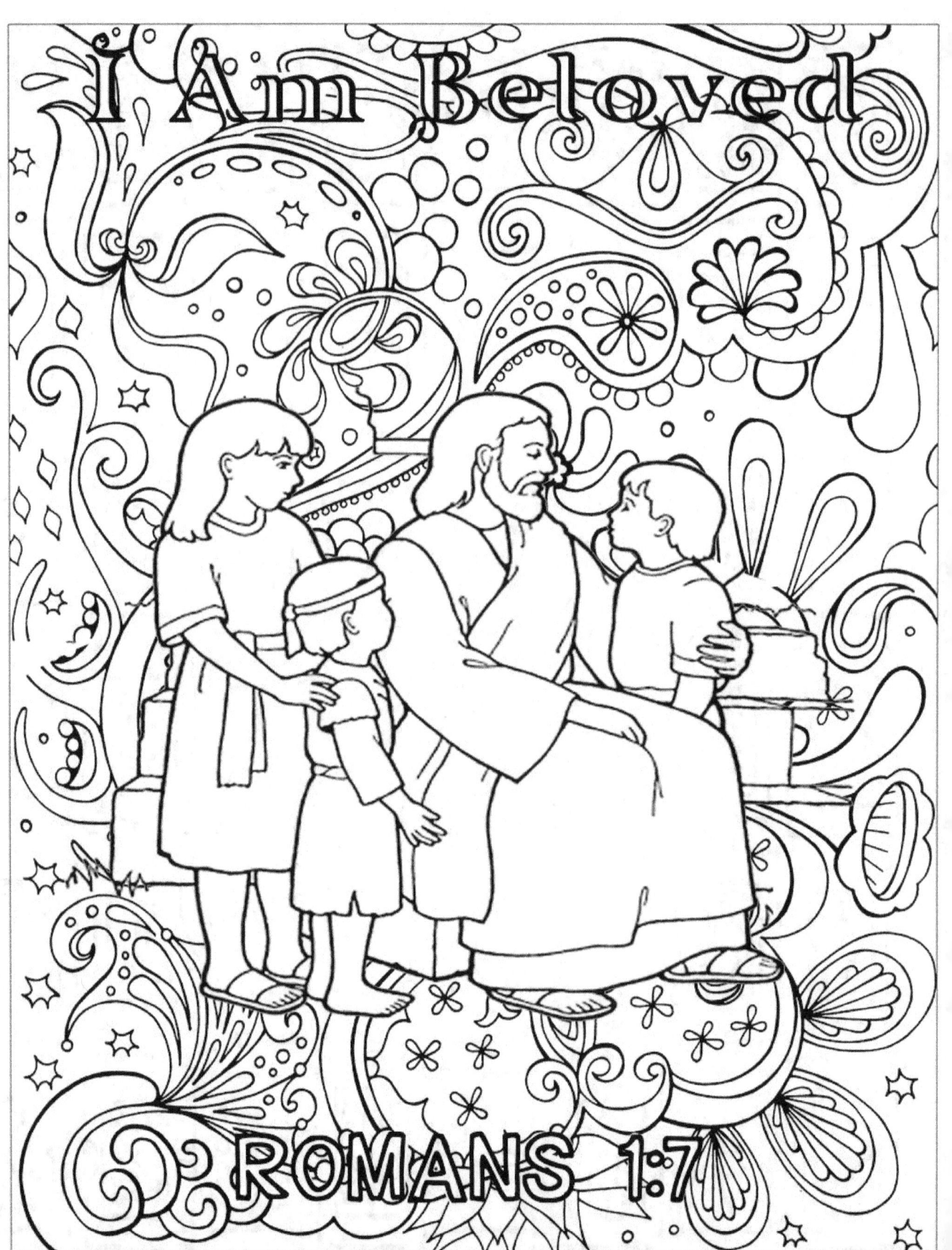

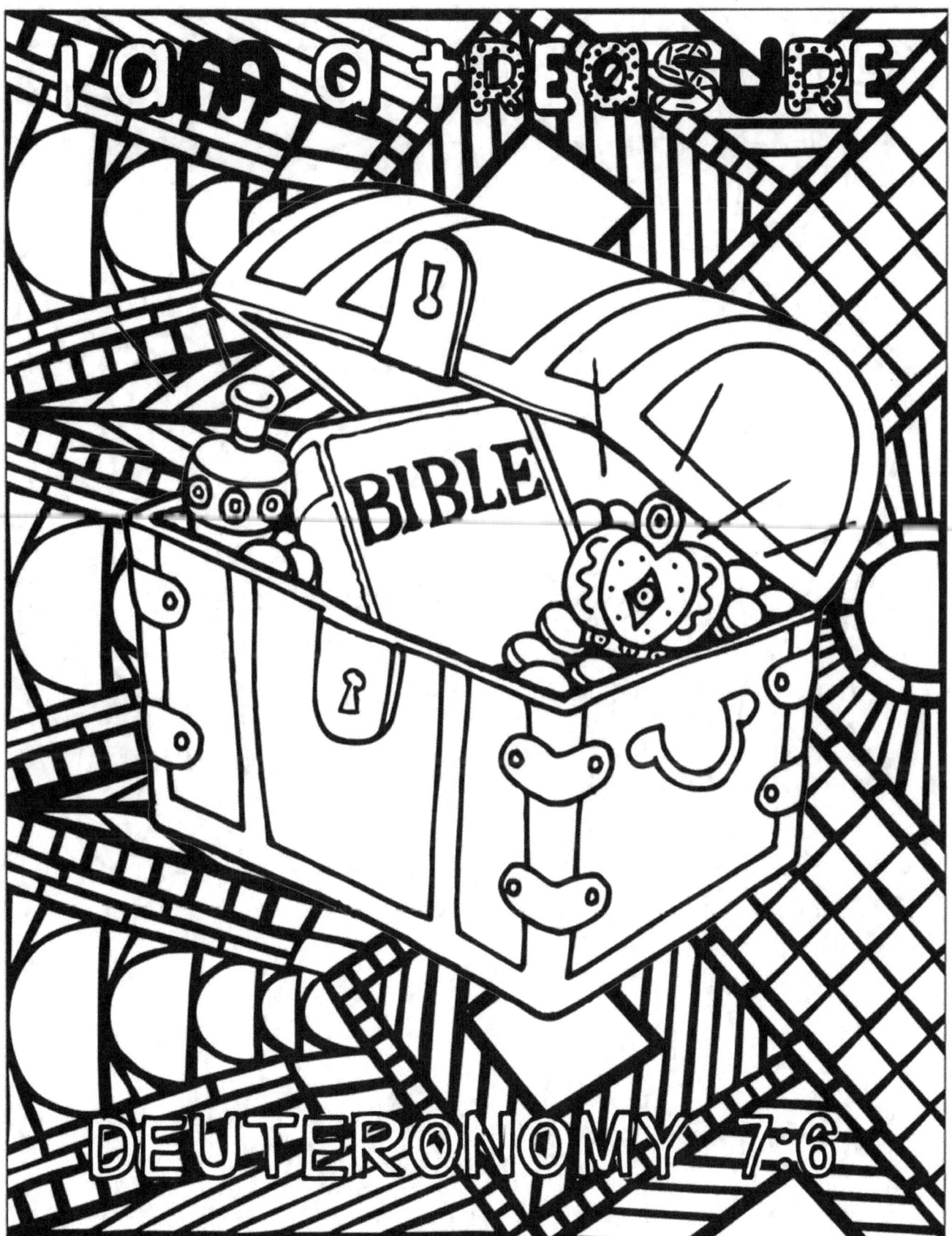

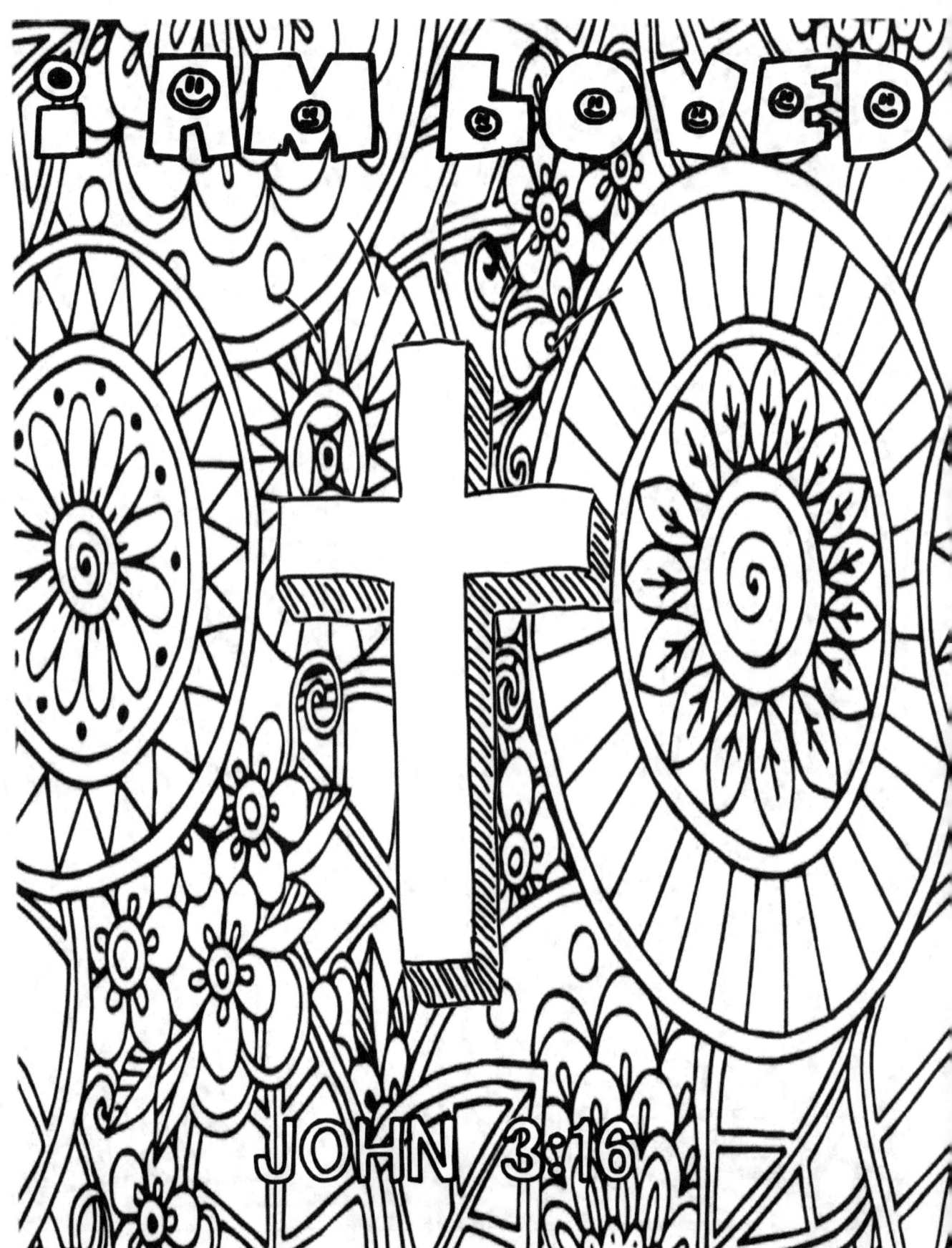

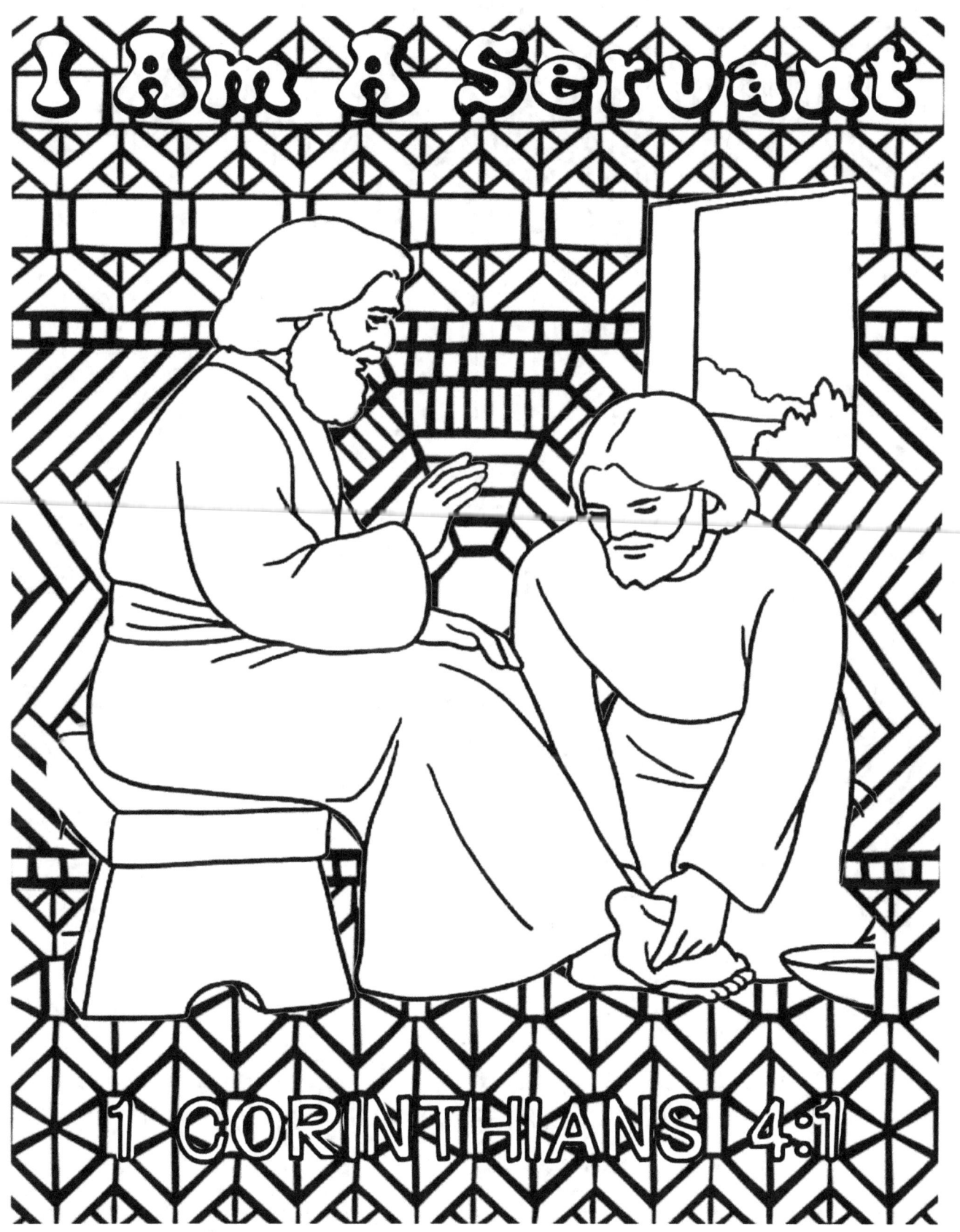

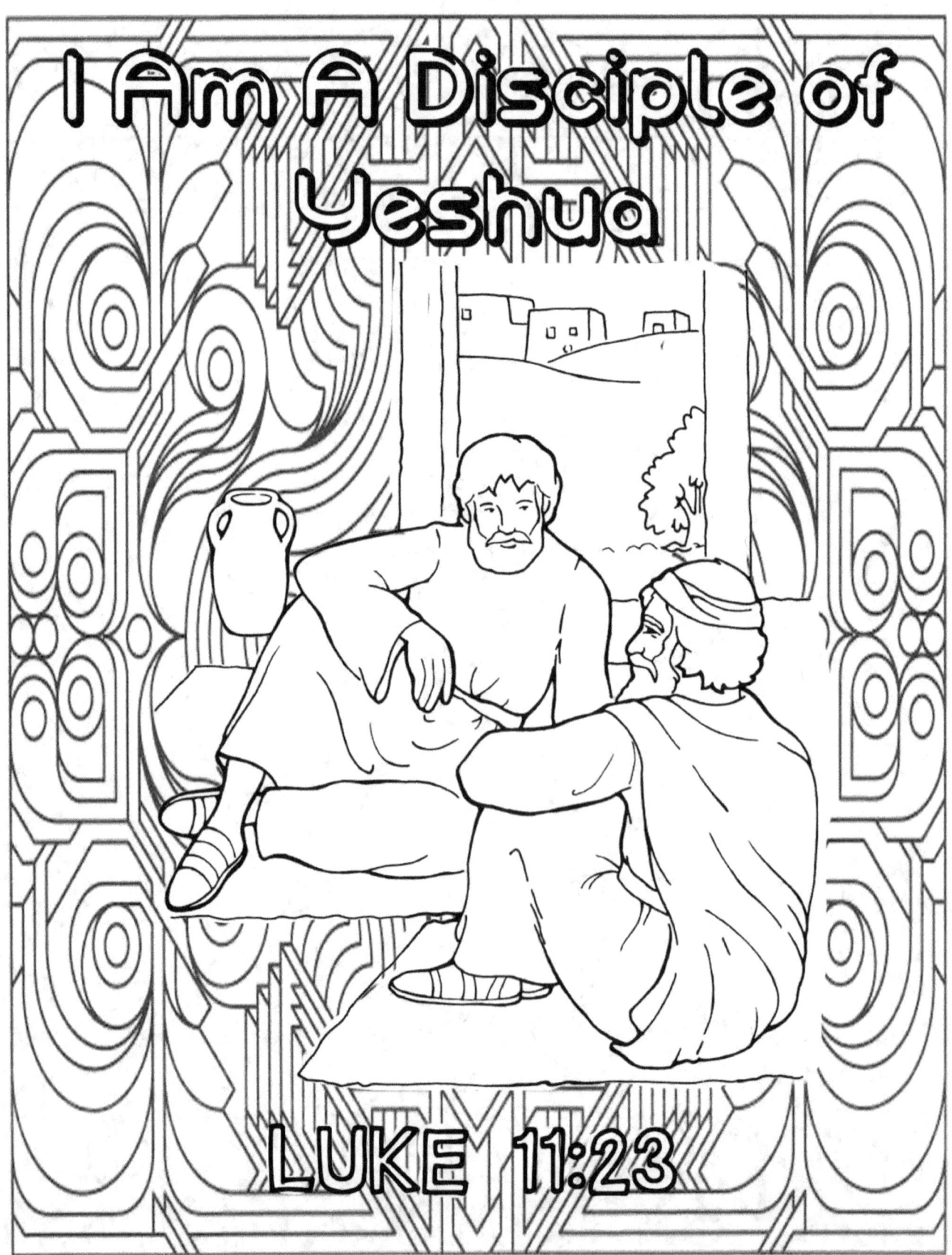

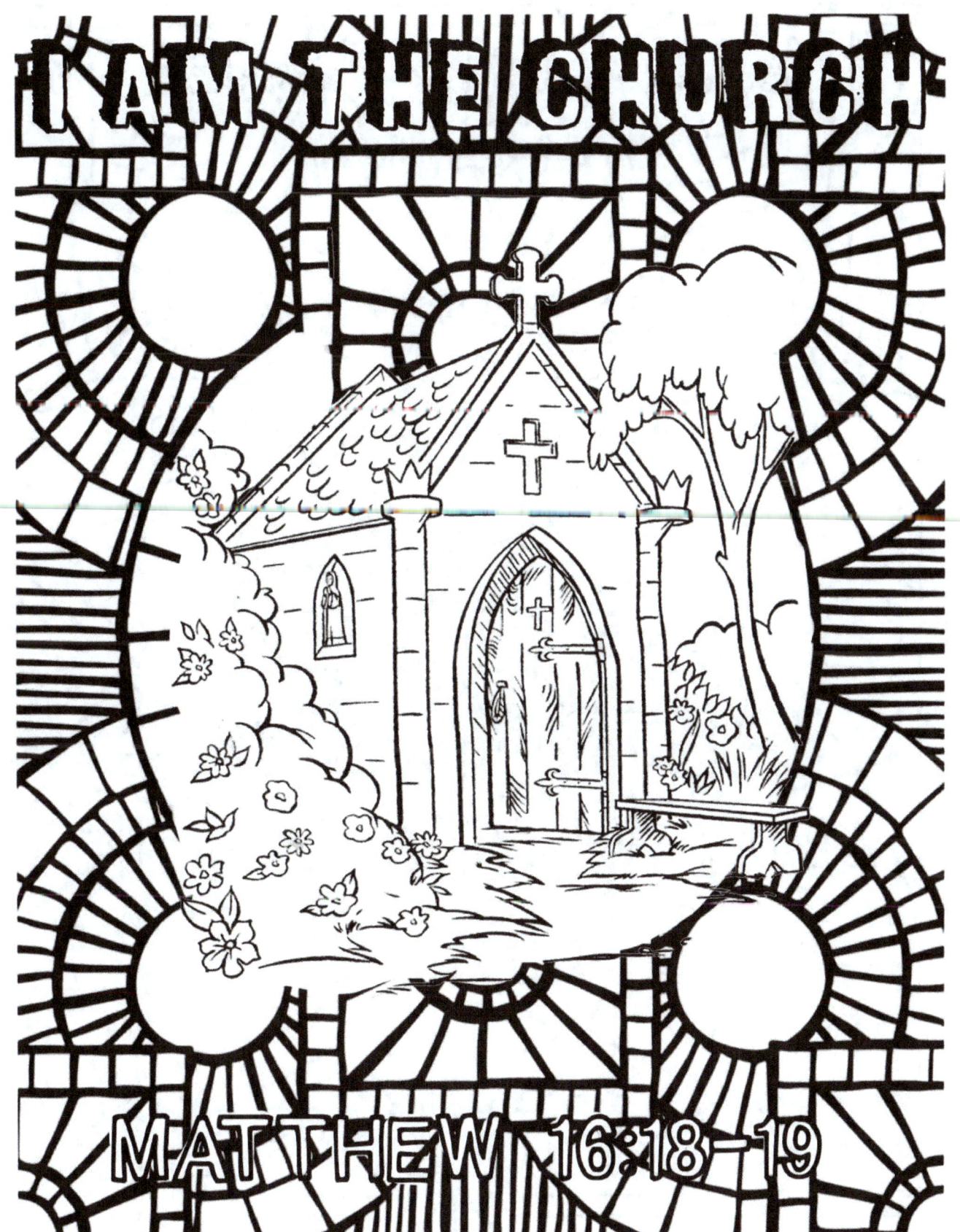

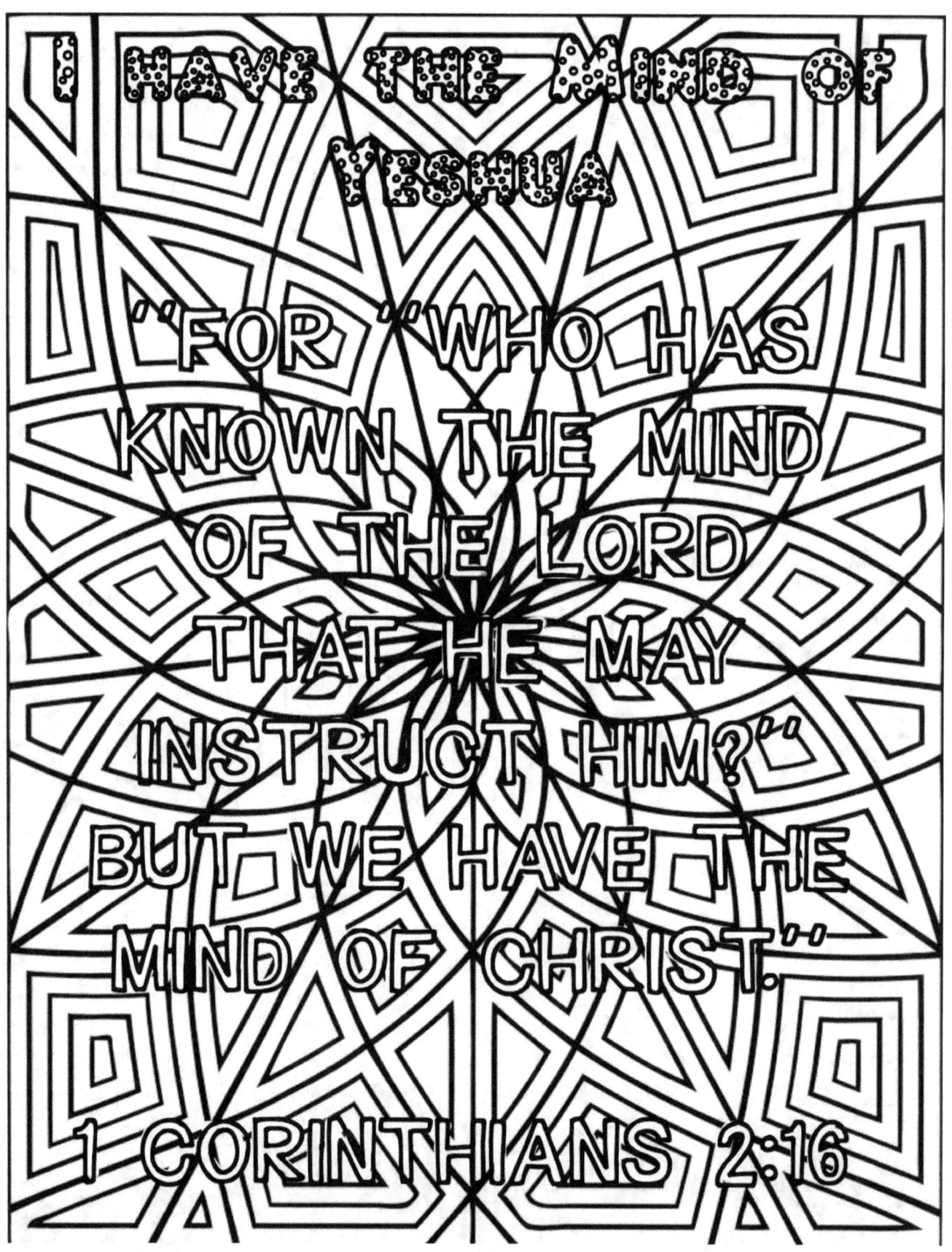

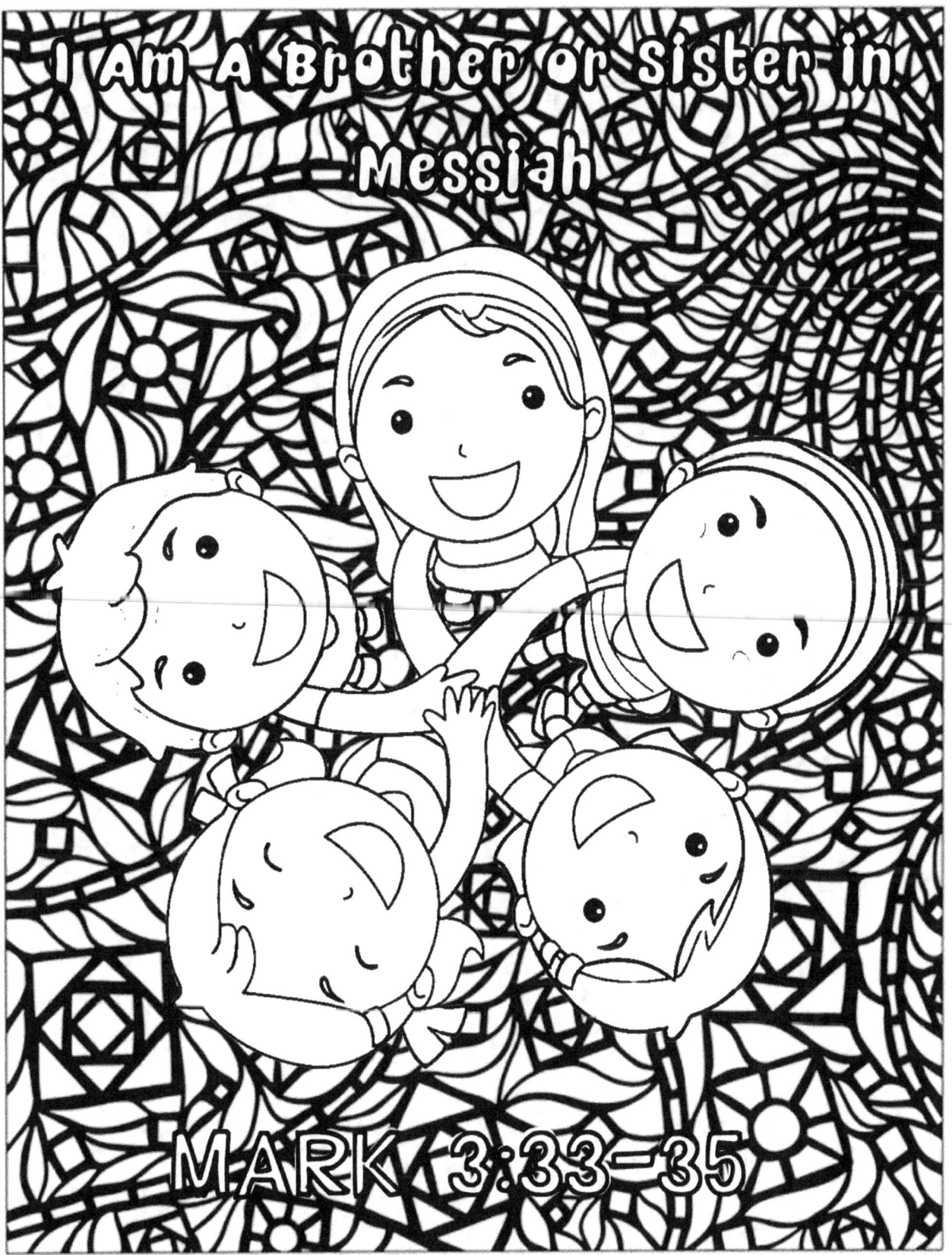

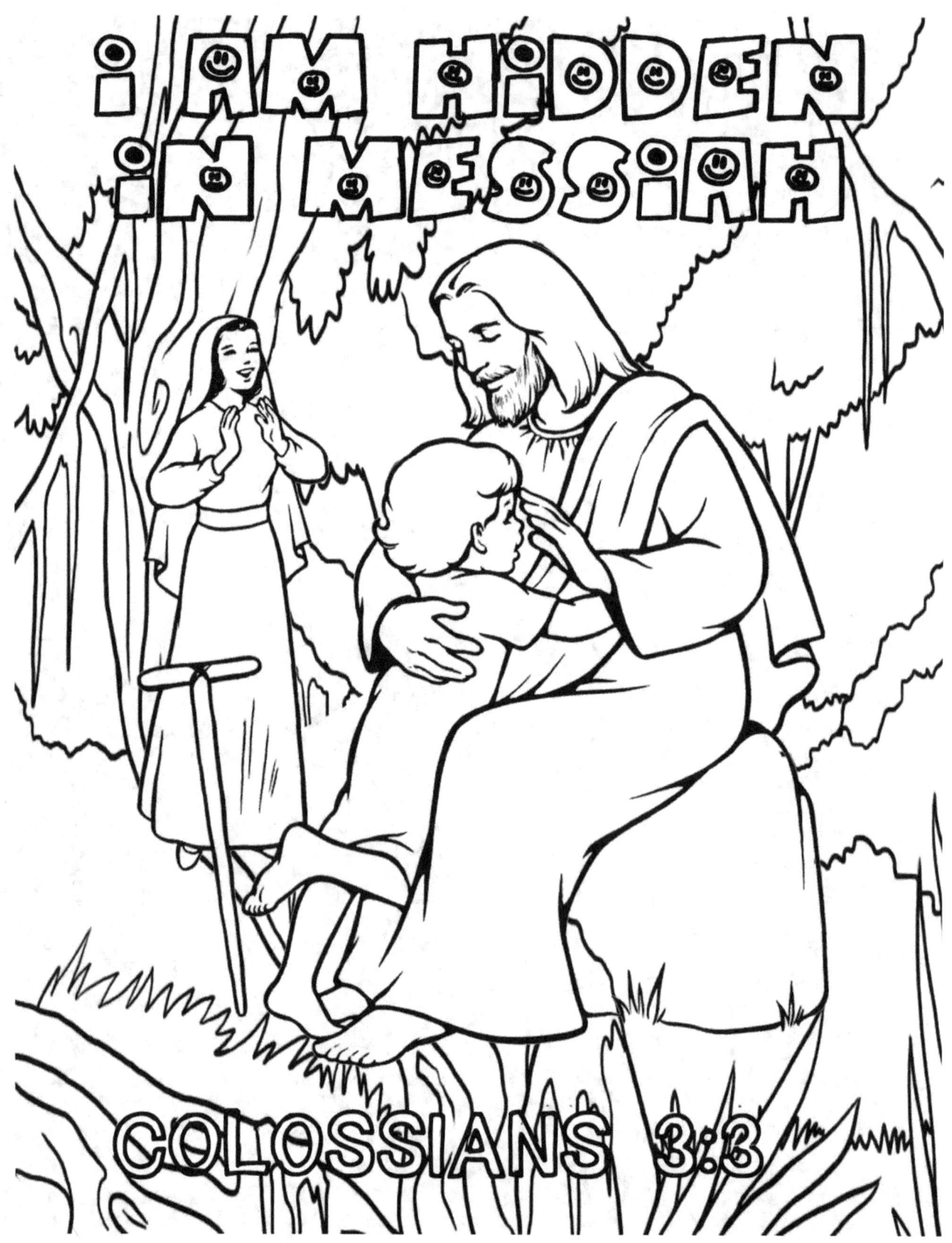

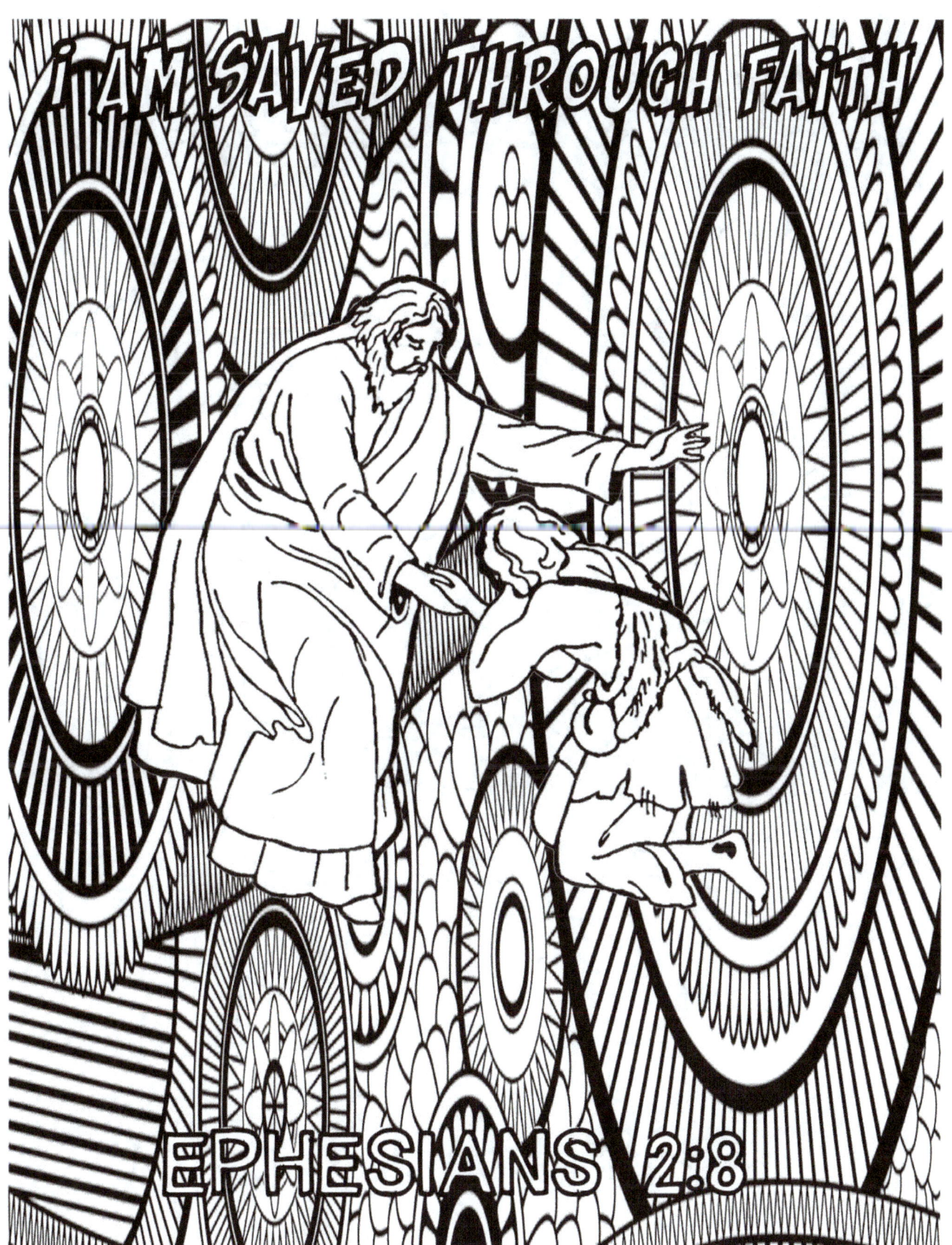

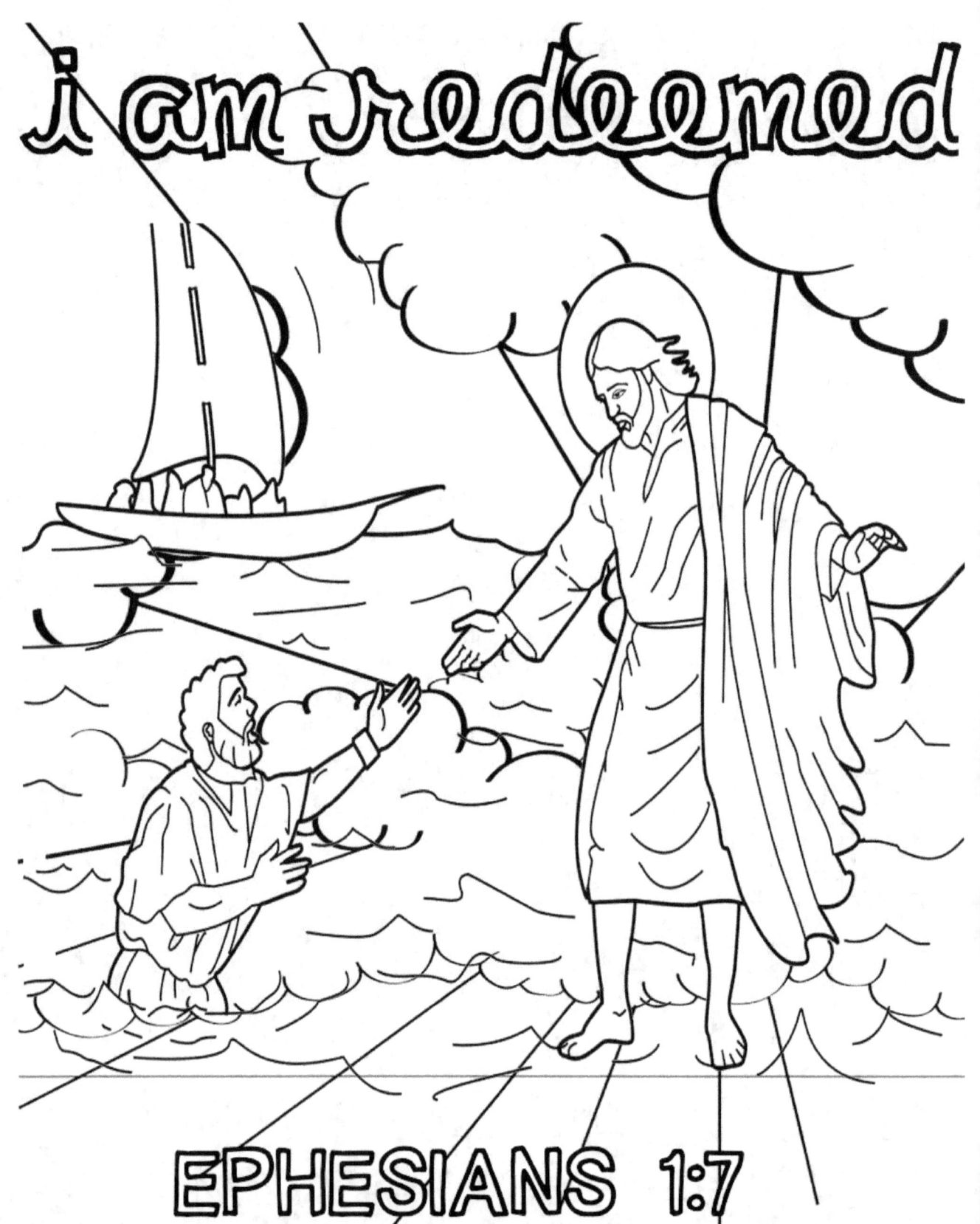

I am His Sheep

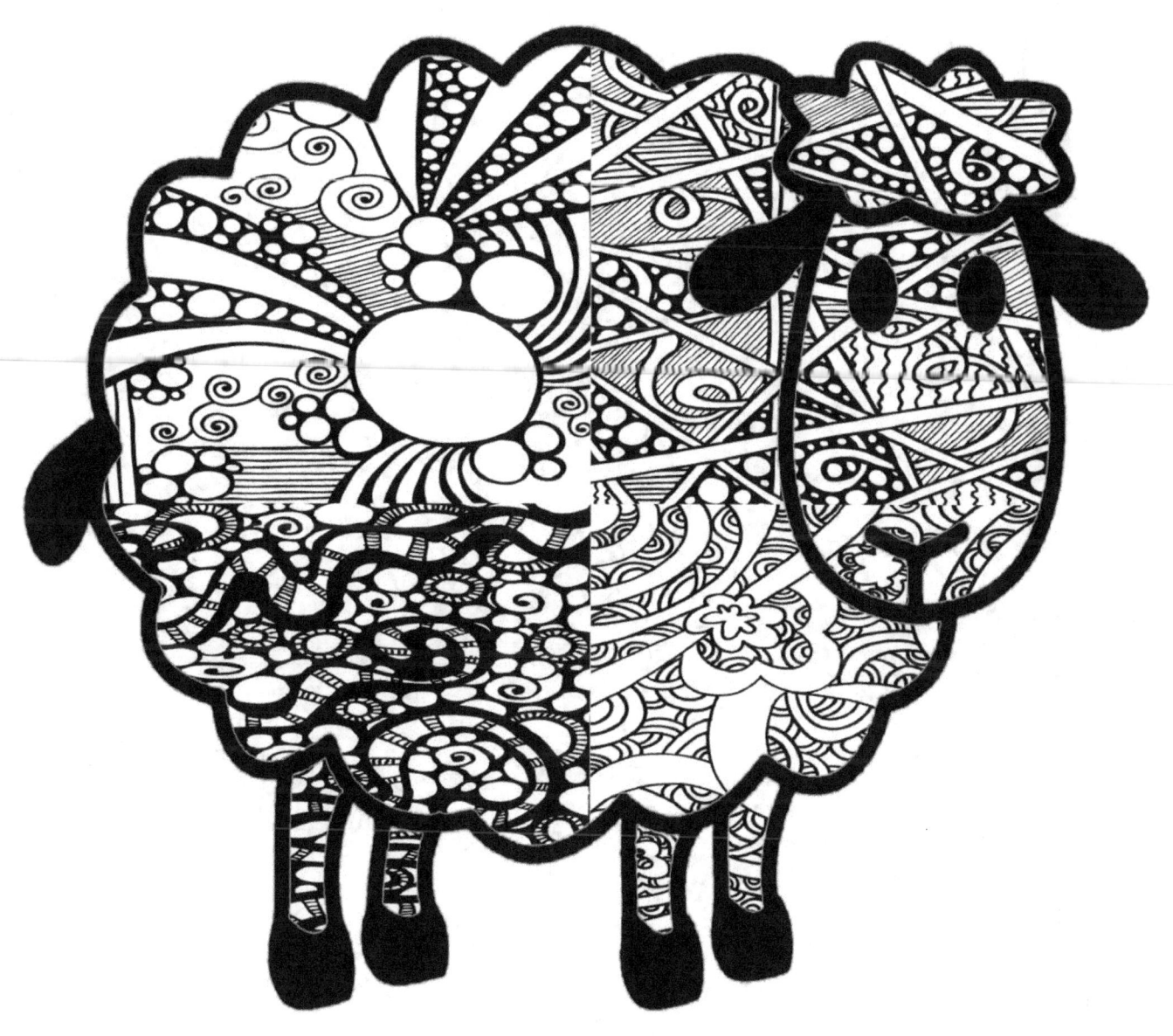

JOHN 10:11

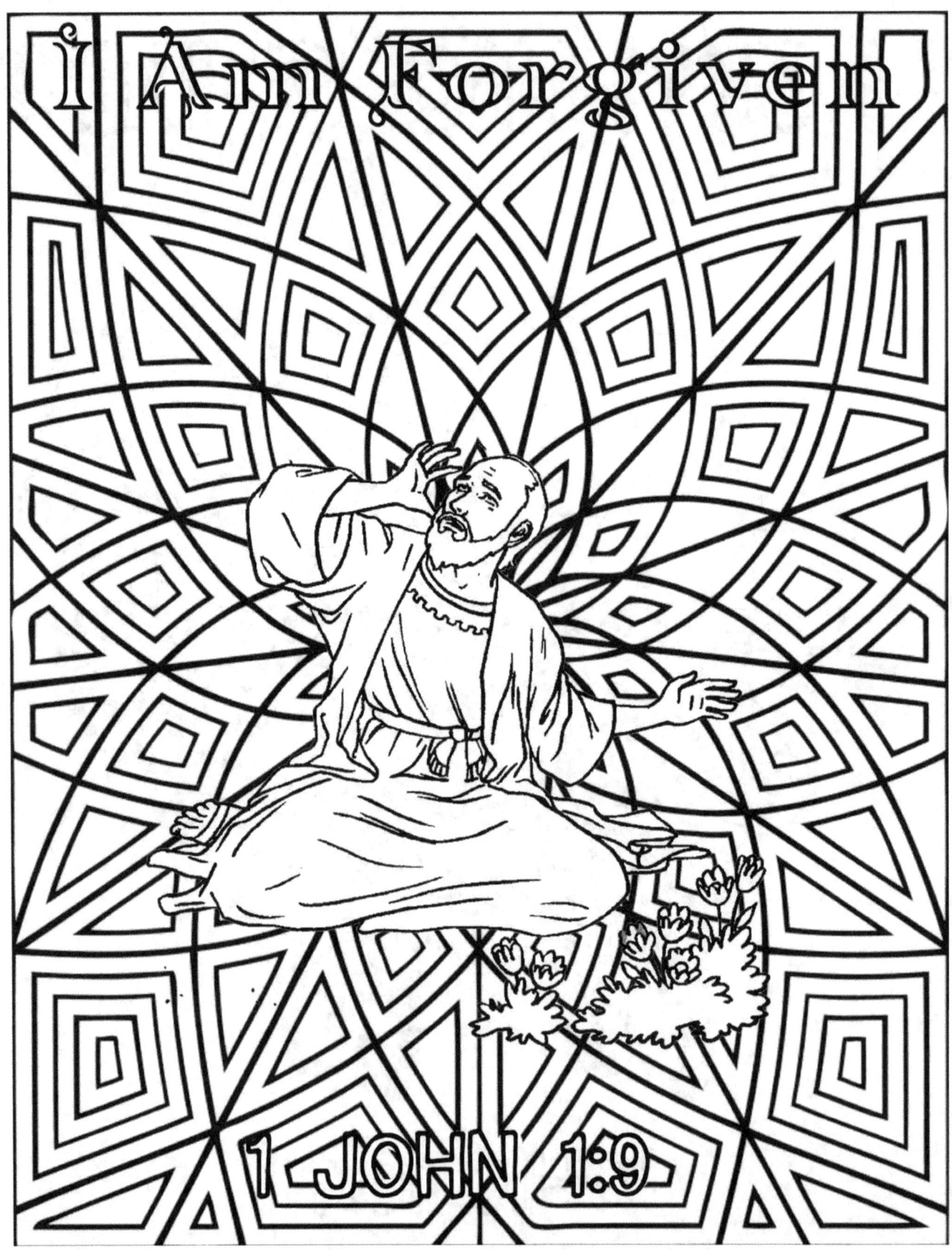

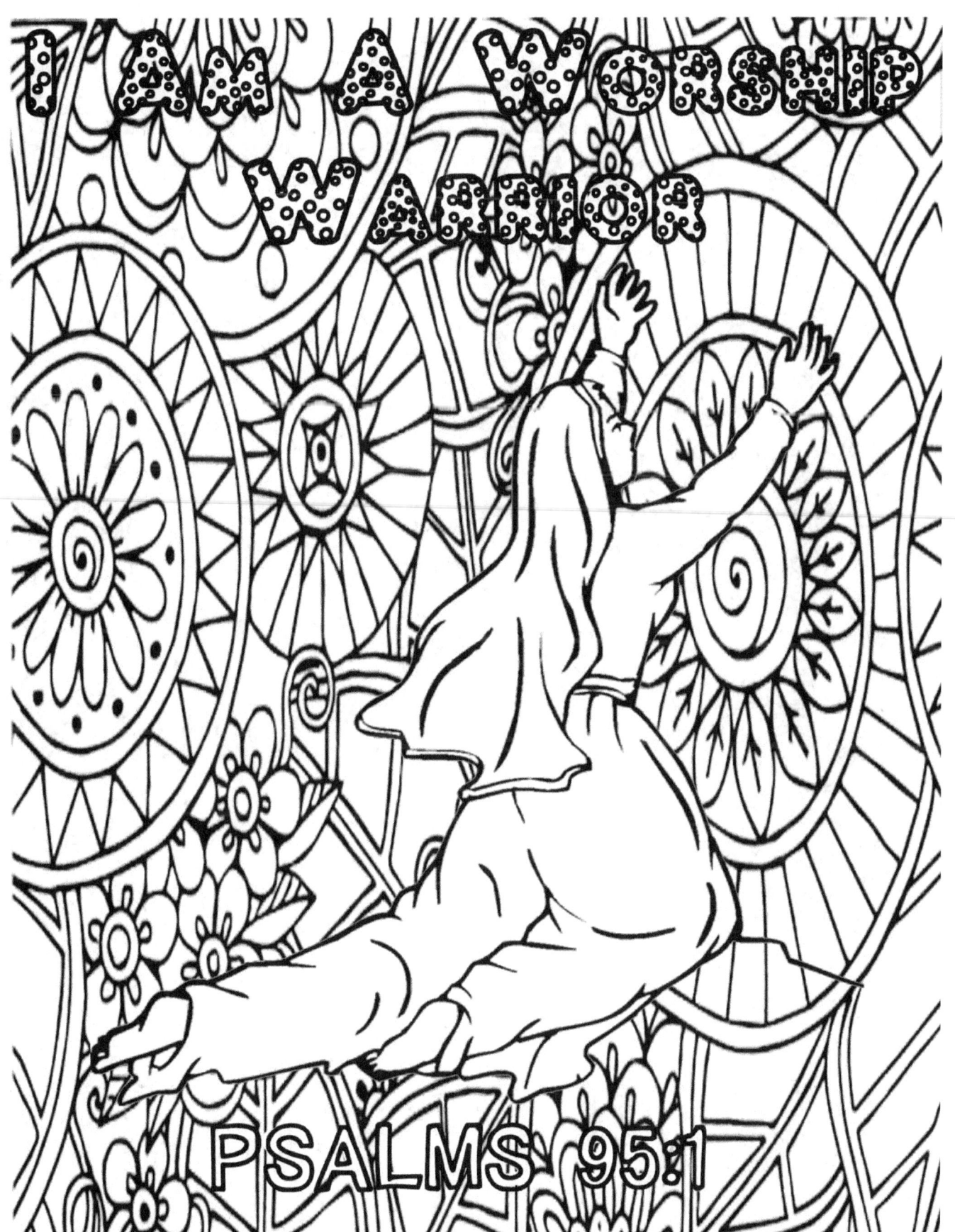

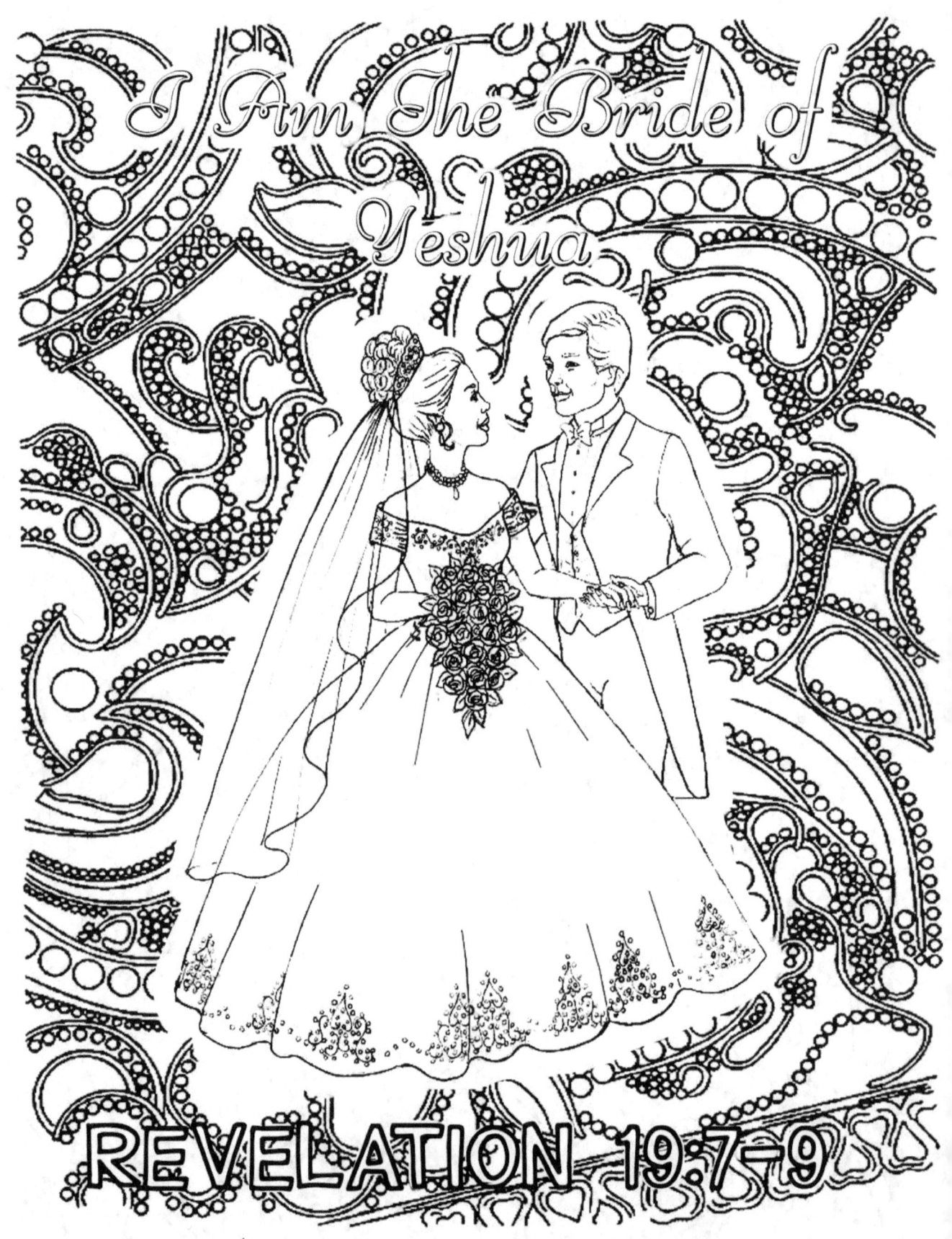

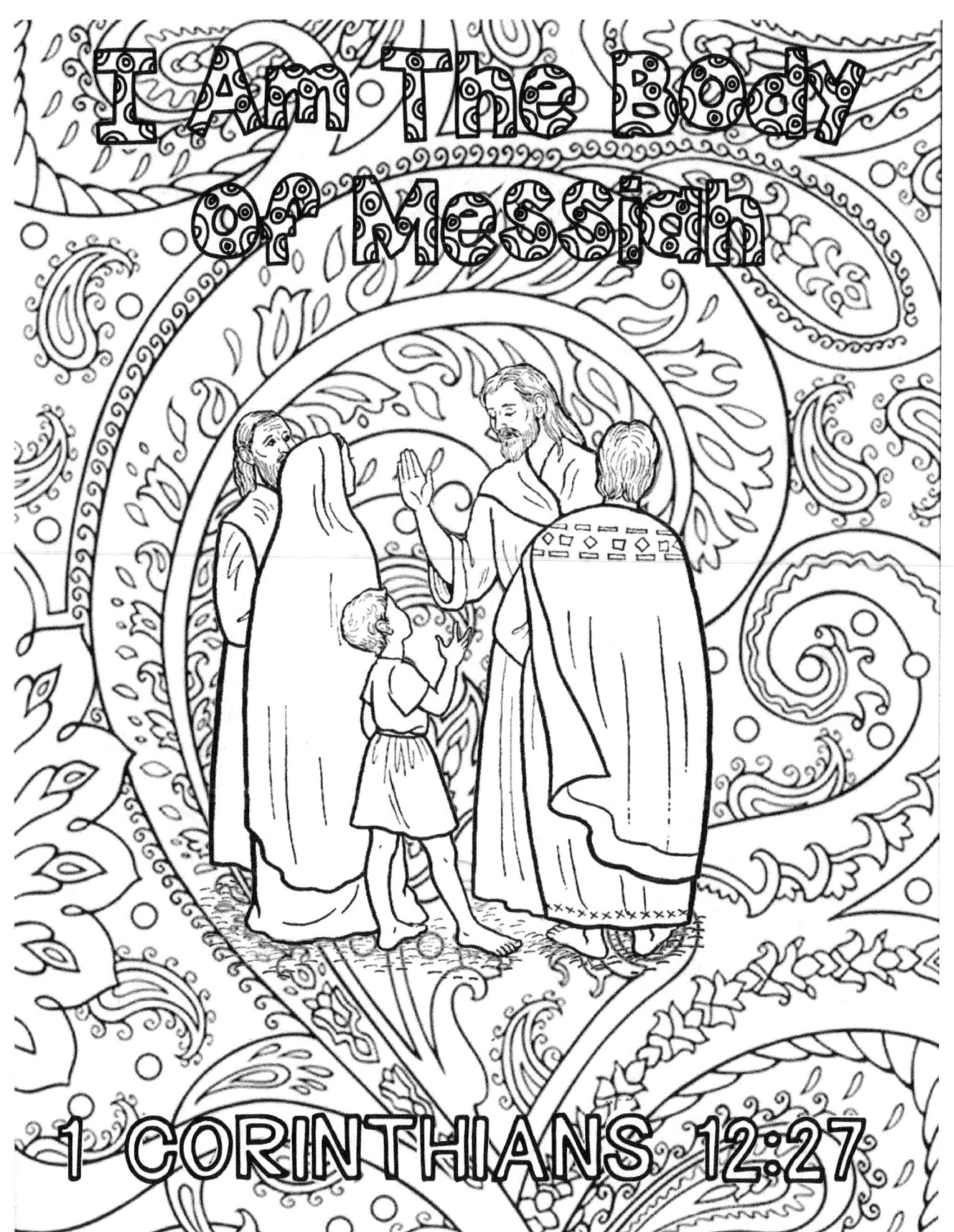

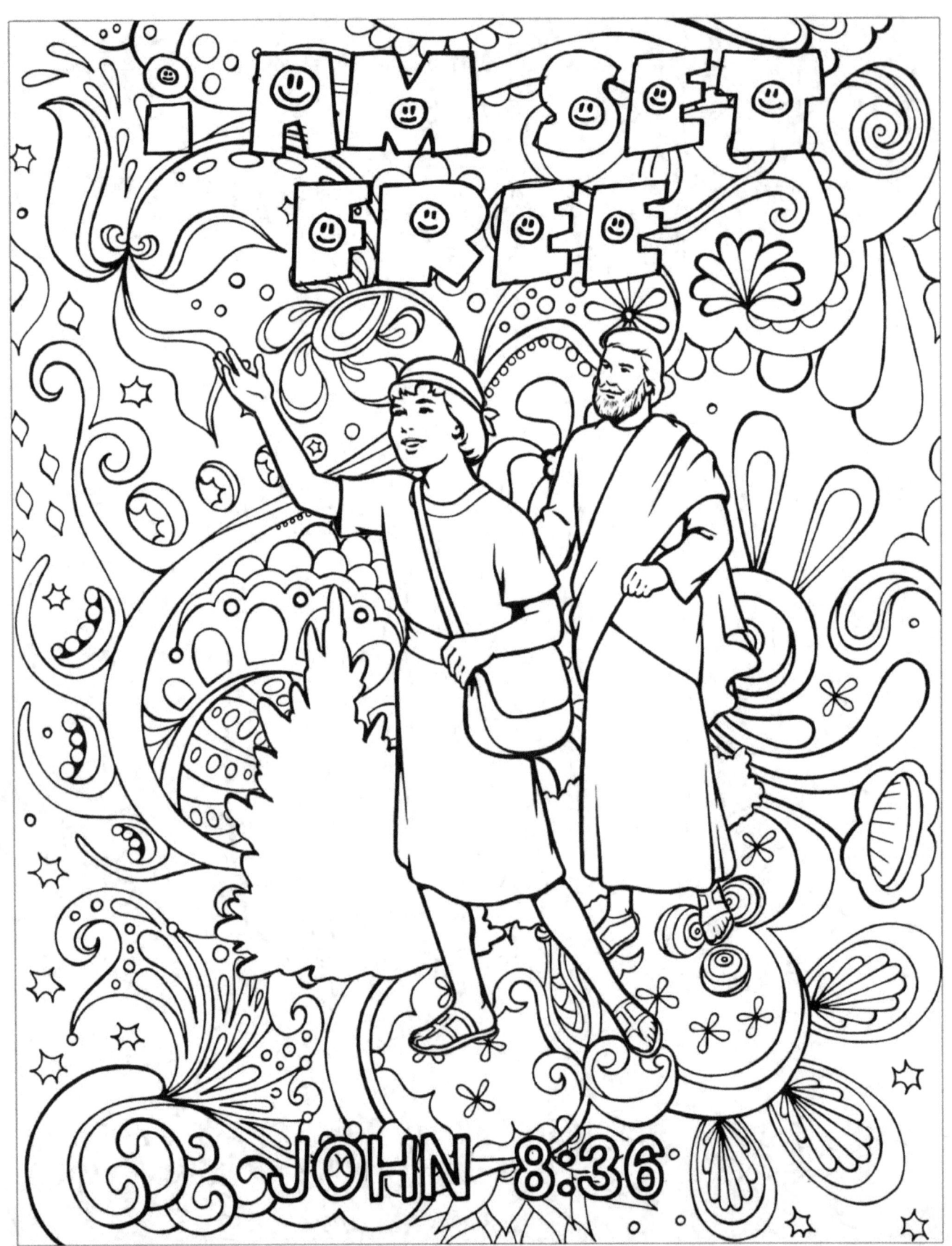

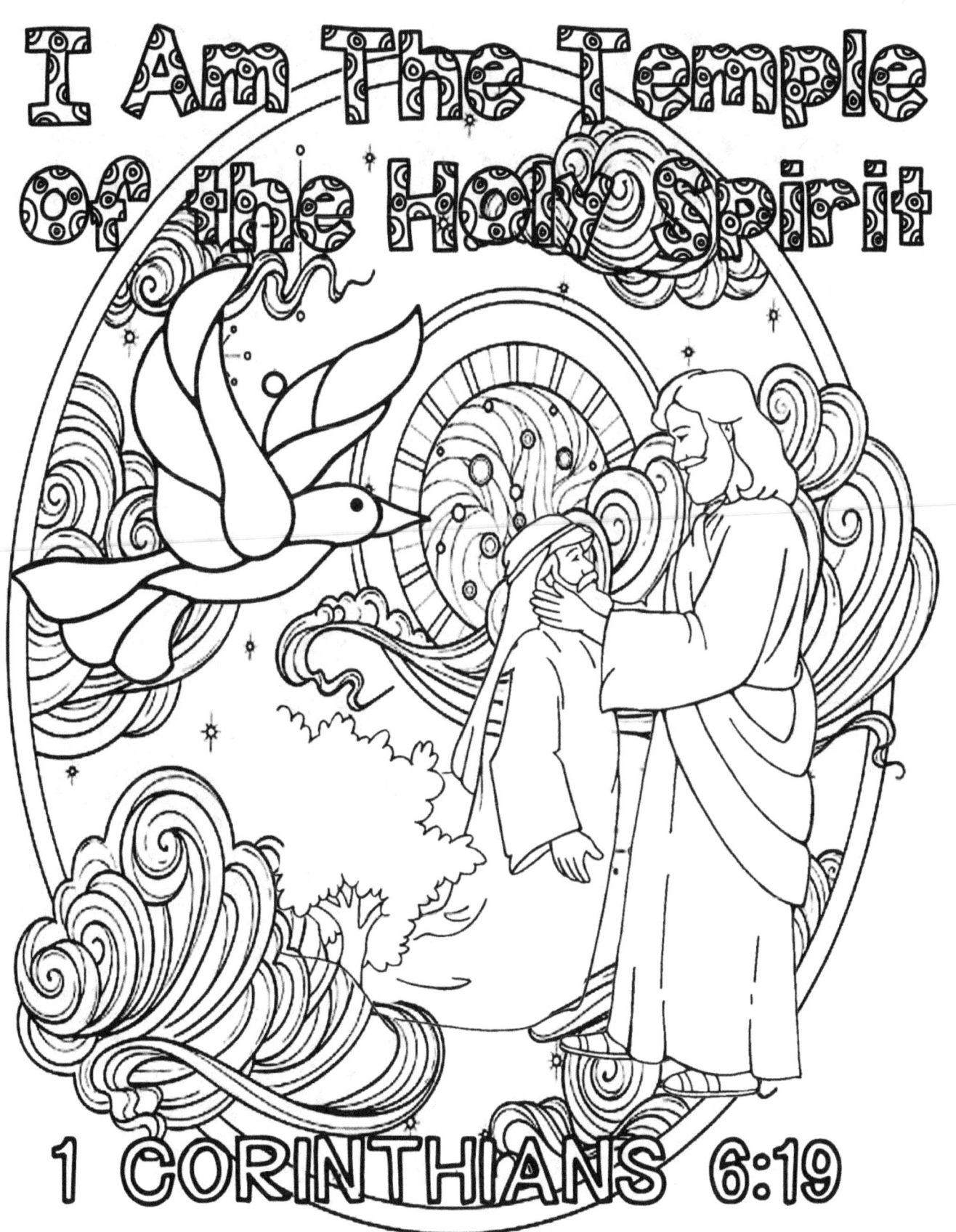

I AM SEALED WITH THE HOLY SPIRIT

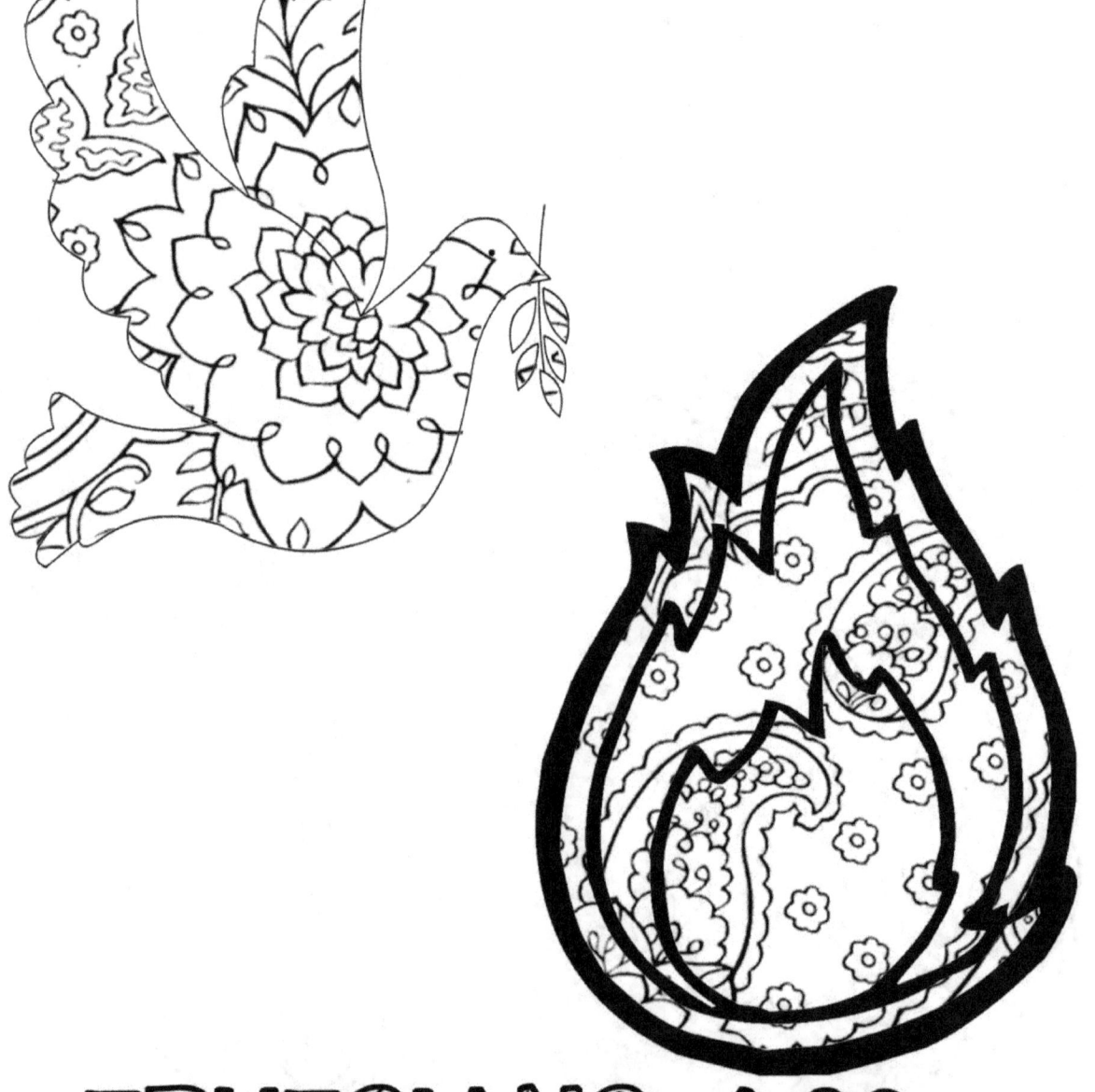

EPHESIANS 4:30

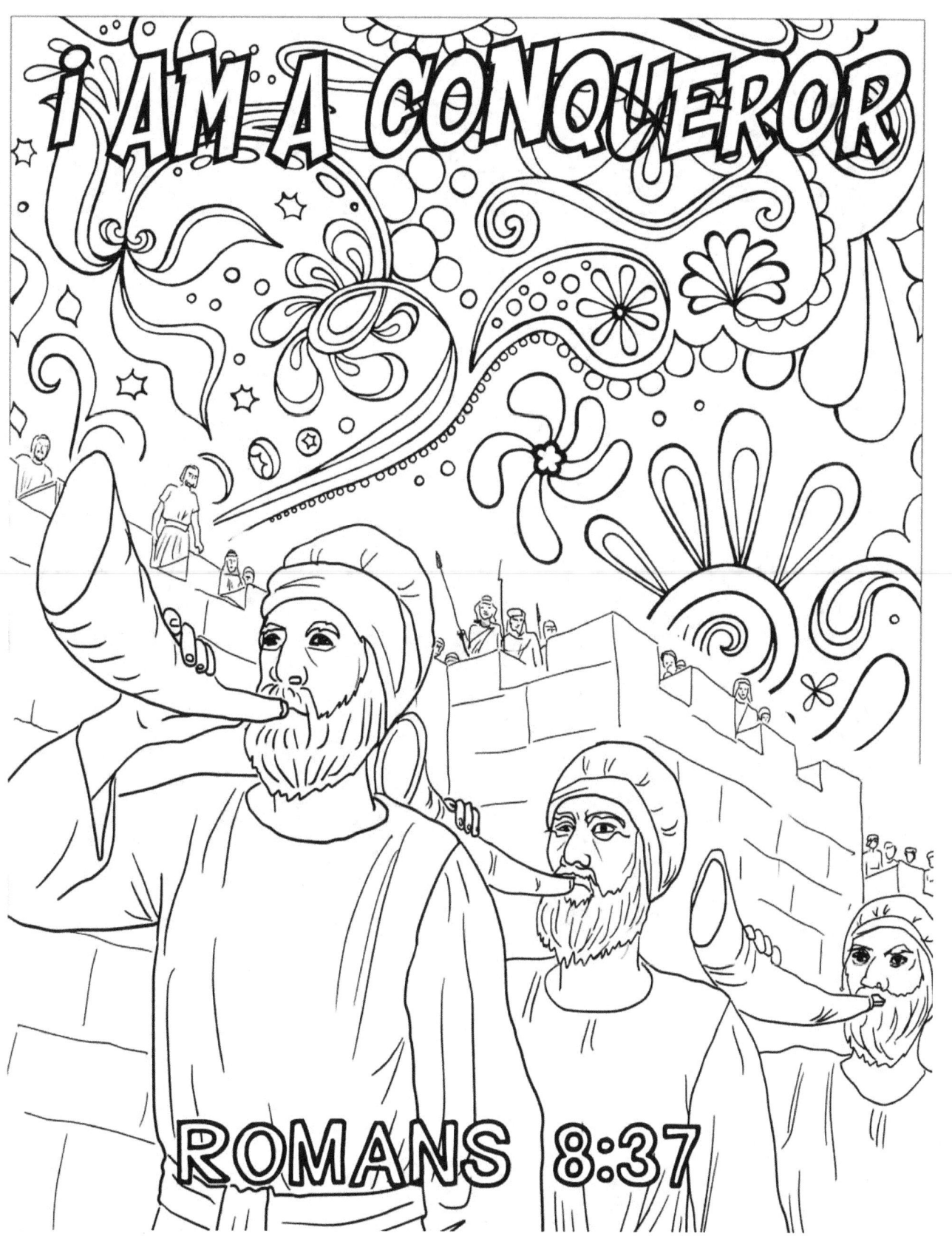

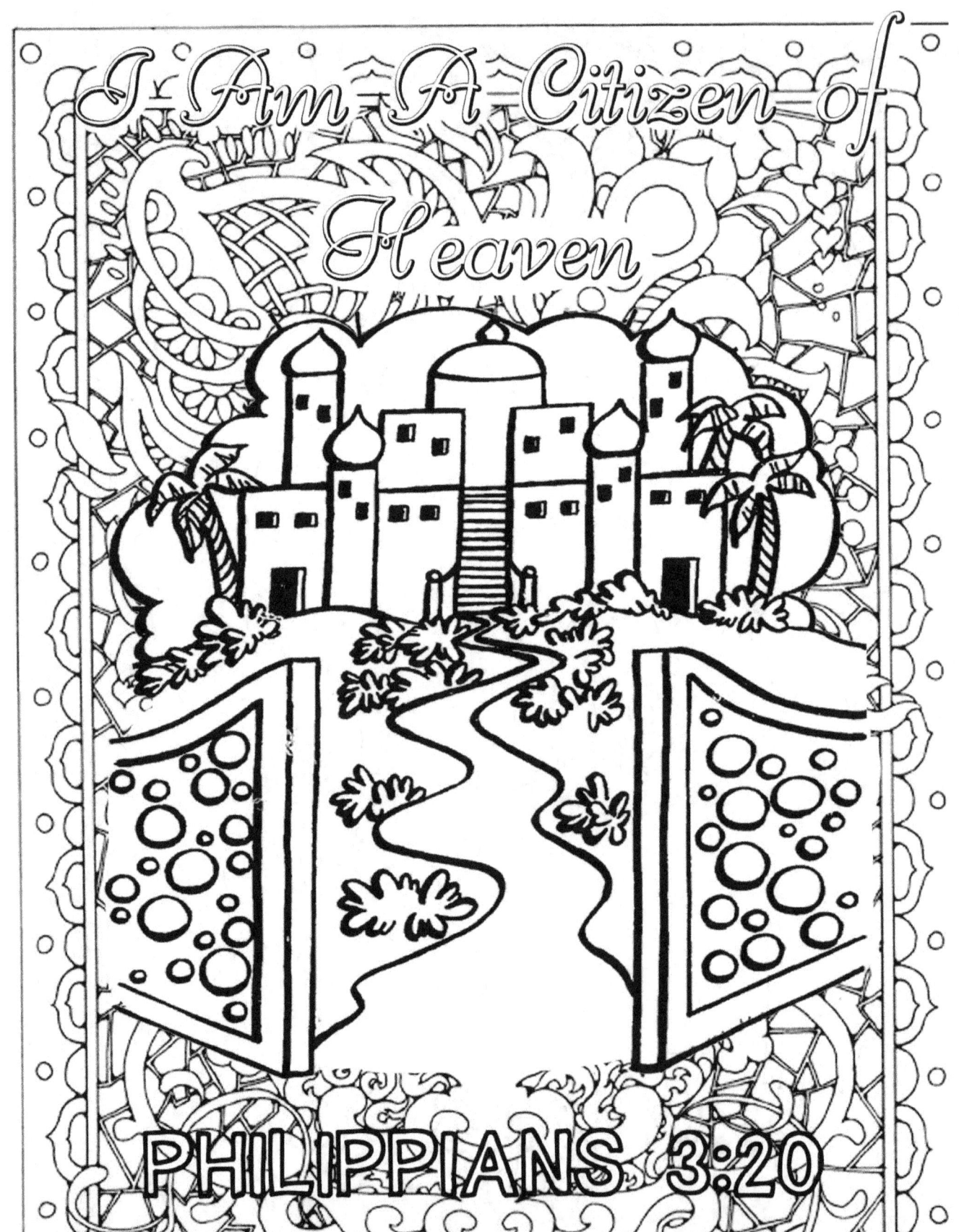

www.ingramcontent.com/pod-product-compliance
Lightning Source LLC
Chambersburg PA
CBHW062126220526
45471CB00010B/3901